And so I began to read ...

Books that have influenced me

Faith Cook

EP BOOKS
1st Floor Venture House, 6 Silver Court, Watchmead,
Welwyn Garden City, UK, AL7 1TS

web: www.epbooks.org

e-mail: sales@epbooks.org

EP Books are distributed in the USA by:
JPL Distribution
3741 Linden Avenue Southeast
Grand Rapids, MI 49548
E-mail: orders@jpldistribution.com
Tel: 877.683.6935

British Library Cataloguing in Publication Data available

ISBN: 978-1-78397-145-9

Printed by Bell and Bain Ltd, Glasgow

To my friend
Rachel Knight
who suggested the theme for this book.

Contents

Before you begin to read ...

aith Cook has written 22 books, largely biographical, and they have influenced a great many people. It has been my privilege to appraise draft manuscripts of several of those books and offer constructive comments. But this twenty-third book is unique. It tells us how Christian books have influenced the author herself and it offers rich insights into how she grew as a Christian under their influence. It does more: it challenges the reader to read (or re-read) the books she refers to. In my own case it challenged me to re-read her own *Grace in Winter: Rutherford in Verse* (Banner of Truth, 1989). With better understanding of what drove her to write it, I read it as if I had never read it before!

This book complements her autobiography *Troubled Journey: A Missionary Childhood in war-torn China* (Banner of Truth, 2004)—

and those who haven't read that book will almost certainly want to do so after reading this one.

This book also reveals two other major literary sources that have strongly impacted her life: the writings of John Bunyan, and Christian hymns that have been written down the ages; here you can gain some insights into how she was impacted. If these insights whet your appetite there are two other volumes you might like to read: *Fearless Pilgrim: the life and times of John Bunyan* (Evangelical Press, 2008), and *Our Hymn Writers and their hymns* (Evangelical Press, 2005).

Meanwhile, enjoy this one.

Ralph E. Ireland
April 2016

JOHN BUNYAN
(After White's pencil drawing in the British Museum)
1628–1928.

At first

And so I began to read. I was almost twenty-one. No, it wasn't as if I had never read before, although, as a child of missionary parents in north-west China, I had quickly learnt that books were a luxury hard to come by. Then with the Sino-Japanese war still raging, books were an even rarer commodity, especially when I became a seven-year-old evacuee child escaping with my school to north India from imminent Japanese capture. Unknown to my parents, our boarding school had been forced to flee in haste for the Japanese army was right at the gates of the small provincial town where the school was situated.

Made up of about twenty-five children aged between seven and eleven, the school had to be accommodated in borrowed buildings set in the foothills of the Himalayas, nestling under the shadow of the mighty Kanchenjunga range. Far from the noise of war, the surroundings were idyllic. And as children we were thrilled to learn that tigers roamed the surrounding jungles—our only grief, of course, was that our parents were far distant.

Scarce treasures

Understandably all books, equipment and even clothing, were in short supply in that remote part of India. This meant that I would read each available book many times over, some becoming great favourites. I even tried to bargain with a member of staff to give me the copy of one she had read to us telling of a lonely wolf that had met a sad death. I offered her a small bookmark I had just made in exchange for *Lobo, the Lone Wolf.* Not surprisingly, I was unsuccessful. However, *The Adventures of Ginger,* a Ladybird book written in appalling doggerel verse about a puppy called Ginger, was my all-time favourite as a seven-year-old. Ginger was born on a farm but sold to a child in London. His mistreatment and eventual escape back to the farm was a story I read and reread until I knew it by heart but still regularly shed tears over the puppy's plight.

Enid Blyton's books were considered unsuitable literature, especially for the children of missionaries, but these I regularly smuggled from a special collection reserved for sick children and read them surreptitiously until my misdemeanours were discovered. Perhaps the most meaningful book of my childhood years was *The Wind in the Willows* by Kenneth Grahame which I read at the age of eleven. Not only did it feed into my love of animals but more importantly it woke my growing sense of the divine. Ratty and Mole's reaction when they caught sight of *The Piper at the Gates of Dawn* could only echo a proper response to a glimpse of the beauty and glory of God.

Then suddenly Mole felt a great awe fall upon him, an awe that turned his muscles to water, bowed his head, rooted his feet to the ground. It was no panic terror—indeed he felt wonderfully at peace and happy … 'Rat!' he found breath to whisper, shaking, 'Are you afraid?'

'Afraid?' murmured the Rat, his eyes shining with unutterable love. 'Afraid of Him? O, never, never! And yet—and yet—O Mole I am afraid.' Then the two animals, crouching to the earth, bowed their heads and did worship.

Clarendon School

After missionaries were peremptorily expelled from China in 1951 following the Communist takeover of the country, our family returned to England. My boarding school in that now distant land was exchanged for a magnificently situated Christian boarding school in North Wales. Even though I was only thirteen and my brother fifteen, my parents wished to return as soon as possible to the Far East, but now to Malaysia instead of China. So Clarendon School became my home and refuge for the next five years of my life.

Although at this point I had access to a wider range of books, our reading material was carefully monitored and largely governed by set books for our state examination timetable. The strong and sincere Christian principles of many members of staff, principles which I quickly absorbed as a young Christian myself, also contributed to my own strictly limited choice of reading material during my teenage years and on into my early twenties.

My understanding of biblical teaching was also limited by the influences that had surrounded me during the formative years of my growth as a Christian. The emphasis was on consistency and godliness among any who claimed to be Christians. Right though this was, it had a strong tendency towards legalism with a constant stress on regulations and forbidden pastimes. I absorbed this emphasis to such an extent that even the reading of a daily newspaper troubled my conscience.

More than this, I made a deliberate decision to forego any reading of novels, including the classics such as Dickens' work, as I found that the sorrows, misfortunes and misdeeds of the characters in the novel gripped my imagination so intensely that it coloured my thinking day and night to an alarming extent. This, to my mind, robbed me of time and energy to think on better things. To children who had had a 'normal' home background and had attended day schools such early legalistic influences would have had far less effect. If I had been mixing with young people from a wide variety of backgrounds I imagine I would have been more able to compare one set of values against another. But in my case the strictures in my thinking that led me to frown on much secular reading were not helpful. When it came to the basic necessity of mixing freely with my peers or of coping with daily life in a broken and troubled world after I had left my highly protected school environment, I found myself at a loss.

Isolation

With school days over, I started at a teacher training college, but found life perplexing and difficult. I had few points of contact with my fellow students and was therefore quickly isolated from general conversation. More than this I was easily shocked at the mind-set and behaviour of others and fell into unattractive self-righteous attitudes—a stance not likely to make me popular! I became lonely and unhappy, and having no parental care or point of refuge with my parents back in Malaysia, my studies suffered in consequence, especially during my first year.

But with college days completed, I took up my first teaching job in a small village school, and found myself gradually forced to lose some of the inhibitions of earlier days. Then in 1957 a change occurred—a change that profoundly influenced my attitudes to the whole of life. It was a revolution that has governed, though not limited, my selection of personal reading material ever since—material to which I shall refer in these pages.

Some of Paul and Faith Cook's collection of treasured books

Changed perspectives

Standing at a bus stop under the flickering light of a street lamp, I was waiting for a bus to take me back to my lodgings. In my hands was a slim book with a lime green cover. The print was small and the light poor. It was not easy to read but it hardly seemed to matter. I was mesmerized. The book, given to me by a friend, was published by a newly-formed company called *The Banner of Truth Trust*, one that I had never heard of before. I had reached page 32 of *The Select Works of Jonathan Edwards*, volume I.

As I read, Edwards told of the occasion when he rode into the woods to pray and 'had a view that for me was extraordinary of the Son of God … and of his wonderful, great, full, pure and sweet grace and love, and meek and gentle condescension,' I was aware that I was standing on holy ground. In those moments I too was being changed. Here was a dimension of spiritual experience that was new to me—one that I longed to know. I continued to read:

> The person of Christ appeared ineffably excellent with an excellency great enough to swallow up all thought and conception— which continued, as near as I can judge, about an hour, which kept me the greater part of that time in a flood of tears and weeping aloud. I felt an ardency of soul to be, what I know not otherwise how to express, emptied and annihilated; to lie in the dust, and to be full of Christ alone; to love him with a holy and pure love; to trust in him, to live upon him, to serve and follow him …

Though faltering in my changing grasp of the possibilities of Christian experience, the life of Edwards gave me dawning understanding of the potentials of spiritual life in terms of knowing and loving Christ himself as a person rather than a mere adherence to a set of rules. It began to control my own praying and desires. As I read more of Jonathan Edward's life I discovered his amazing 'seventy resolutions' all written before his twentieth birthday. I copied many into my private notebook, words such as 'Resolved, Never to give over, nor in the least slacken my fight against my corruptions, however unsuccessful I may be.' Or, alternatively 'Resolved, Whenever I do any conspicuously evil action, to trace it back, till I come to the original cause; and then, both carefully endeavour to do so no more, and to fight and pray with all my might against the original of it.' And then I came

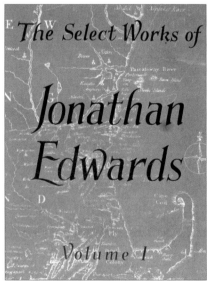

across this resolution which so frightened and challenged me that it still remains with me, though I first read it over fifty years ago. 'Resolved, That I will live so as I shall wish I had done when I come to die.'

With my own twenty-first birthday approaching, the only gifts I now asked for were more books from this publishing company. Before long I proudly displayed a small row of new books in my room. Some had strange titles such as *A Body of Divinity* by Thomas Watson. Most formed demanding reading, some I read a little at a time while others did not receive the attention they deserved. But my horizons were widening and with them new understanding and liberty of thought.

A surprising preacher

The preaching that now attracted me echoed these same longings and I would travel up to London as often as I could to hear such preaching. Occasionally student preachers took the services at the local church where I now had my membership. One particular student from Spurgeon's College attracted considerable comment from the congregation. Some felt his preaching was both searching and challenging. Others felt it was unnecessarily severe and demanding. I fell into this latter category. When this young preacher, whom I judged to be a number of years older than me, returned to preach some months later I was surprised, perhaps even shocked, that he once again chose to take the same passage of Scripture to preach on as before. Christ, he told us in no uncertain terms, commanded his disciples to deny themselves, take up their cross daily and follow him. Armed with my new theological interests gained from some of my reading, I had the temerity to ask the preacher a question at the end of the service: a short conversation followed—a conversation which, I later discovered, had not passed unnoticed.

The student preacher was offered hospitality at the home of some close friends of mine, and there we met once again. But not until I received an unexpected packet in the post a few days later did I realize the significance of this particular contact. Bemused, I opened the envelope and discovered a small blue booklet inside with another strange title: *Things Most Surely Believed Among Us*. Recently republished and priced at one shilling and sixpence, this was the Baptist Confession of Faith of 1689.

In other words it was a catechism listing all the tenets of faith held by the early Baptists—a strange choice with which to woo a young lady. Turning to the preface I read:

> Be not ashamed of your faith; remember it is the ancient gospel of martyrs, confessors, reformers and saints. Above all it is the truth of God against which the gates of hell cannot prevail.

The gift was swiftly followed by a proposal of marriage a week or two later—a proposal I eventually accepted when I had recovered from the shock. Paul and I were married in April 1961 after waiting some eighteen months for my parents to return to England for their regular four-yearly home assignment from Malaysia where they were serving in one of the new resettlement villages created to protect the people after the Second World War.

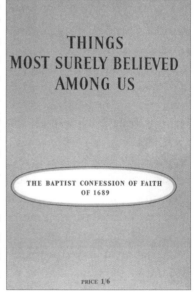

With a deep concern for the north of England, then with little gospel witness, Paul had accepted a call to become pastor of a small church in the county town of North Yorkshire, Northallerton. A struggling newly-established cause, the church had a membership of fifteen to twenty at the most, some little more than nominal in their Christian commitment. This town became our first home.

A common interest

With my marriage I was introduced to a staggering wealth of books. I soon found that books were a factor which bound us together in a common interest. On our honeymoon and each successive holiday we were drawn almost magnetically to small second-hand book shops with volumes old and new stacked crazily on shelving reaching to the ceiling. The smell of old books had a haunting appeal and many happy hours were spent searching out these treasures. Soon every corner in our small Northallerton Manse was crammed with books; they spilled over into bedrooms, living rooms, and had not our kitchen and bathroom been too small, they doubtless would also have accommodated the ever-growing collection. And as if this were not enough, Paul became the first British agent of the American *Presbyterian and Reformed Publishing Company,* importing their titles into England. Regular postal vans would draw up and deposit yet more books in our hall to be piled up in odd corners awaiting distribution.

Paul's influence finally broke my taboos about any secular reading, but more importantly I was gradually introduced to some of the great theologians of the Christian church. The names of men such as B. B. Warfield and Louis Berkhof became household words. But it was to Herman Bavinck's heart-warming, *Our Reasonable Faith* that I responded with real delight. Yet even back in those days it was to history and biography that I turned most readily.

The Reformation in England

One highly readable book stands out above all others: J. H. Merle d'Aubigné's history of *The Reformation in England*. The first handsome volume, was republished in 1962 by *The Banner of Truth Trust* from the 1853 version. It was all I could have wished for in excitement, adventure and courage—and all packed into the incredible story of the Christian church in England during the period known as the Reformation. Thinking back, I now realize it was that volume, and volume 2, published the following year, which awoke in me a love of biography that would lead on in later years to my own recording of the lives of heroes and heroines of the church of Jesus Christ—forgotten men and women from whose lives we can learn so much.

I read of John Wycliffe's lonely stand for truth as he gave us an early translation of the Scriptures and of the fearful sufferings visited on his followers in consequence. But it was William Tyndale's life that caught my imagination as he steadfastly pursued his solitary work of translating the Scriptures into the beautiful English that formed the basis for our own Authorized Version of the Bible and the shape of the English language itself. And his earthly reward? betrayal, imprisonment in a dank dungeon, strangling and then burning at the stake. I was astonished, indignant and angry in turns, yet knew that his true reward was far different.

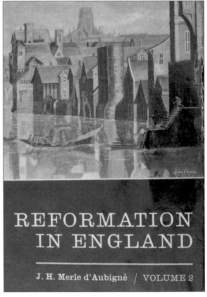

REFORMATION
IN ENGLAND

J. H. Merle d'Aubigné / VOLUME 2

When the frivolous Anne Boleyn, second wife of Henry VIII, received a beautifully bound copy of Tyndale's New Testament, a gift from

Tyndale himself, in all likelihood it led to her conversion. With her natural eager and vivacious nature she began to encourage the reformation of the Church—perhaps without sufficient discretion or consideration of Henry's fickle temperament. Before long the king tired of Anne and resented the fact that she had not given him his longed-for male heir. Soon his roving eye spotted the quiet and attractive Jane Seymour. Anne's days were numbered. She continually protested her innocence as trumped-up charges of adultery were levelled against her, but inevitably she would face a cruel death at the hands of the public executioner—Henry's easiest way of ridding himself of unwanted wives. The end was truly heroic. She begged the forgiveness of those whom she had wronged and freely forgave the King who had so fearfully wronged her. Crying out, 'O Jesus, receive my soul,' Anne was delivered from the treachery of an earthly monarch and embraced in the arms of a heavenly King.

The story of the martyrs was no less harrowing and astonishing as d'Aubigné turned names in the history books into real people with real emotions. We read of Thomas Bilney's anguished recantation of his faith in order to save his life, his consequent despair and then his renewed courage as he faces the stake in Norwich—a story reminiscent of a twentieth-century sufferer, Wang Ming Dao of China whose faith ultimately triumphed despite an earlier failure.

Benefits of reading biography

Reading Christian biography has had a major effect on my Christian life. Before my marriage I had read little and had only the haziest idea of church history. Never have I forgotten how shocked Paul was to discover that I, his fiancée, did not even recognize John Wesley when we came across the waxwork of him as we walked around Madame Tussauds.

So not only did d'Aubigné's account fascinate and challenge me, it provided a starting point on which to build a far better understanding of church history. Nor was it a merely dry intellectual exercise, for it provided a unique part in giving me an overview of God's faithful dealings with his people in the past. And as he is the unchanging God, he still leads, rebukes and encourages his people in similar ways today. As readers we learn what nurtured and sustained former Christians from day to day, what mistakes they made, how God often brought good even out of their folly and failure. We are humbled by the great sufferings some endured for the gospel's sake and see how such afflictions led to greater endurance and godliness. As we learn how these believers pleaded in prayer for God's mercies and received answers from heaven to their petitions, we are encouraged to believe that the same God will hear our prayers. By reading of the way many found grace to die triumphantly, trusting in Christ to take them through death and into his glory, we can be delivered from the nagging fear of death. And as if this were not enough, such accounts also add valuable significance and encouragement to the part that we too can play in our own generation in God's overarching purposes.

When reading time is scarce

*H*owever great the encouragement to persevere with reading more Christian biography I may have derived from J. H. Merle d'Aubigné's account of the *Reformation*, my days of opportunity for such reading were dramatically reduced with the arrival of our first child, Esther. Such periods are demanding enough for any young mother, but with my total lack of any earlier experience of home life and my parents currently serving as missionaries far off in Malaysia, I found these days particularly stressful. I still attempted to read but discovered the only possible time was while nursing the baby. With a small lectern set up in front of me, I would open my book.

My first choice was a massive volume, one of four, each measuring eleven inches by nine—an autobiography of C. H. Spurgeon compiled from his letters, diary and other records by his wife Susannah.

Intriguing reading, it was nevertheless an unfortunate choice as now and then there would be a massive clatter as one of Paul's precious Spurgeon volumes crashed to the floor—no easy trial for my careful husband. Nevertheless, I did master all four volumes and it proved fascinating reading and particularly helpful as I began to understand the privileges and challenges both of family life and the responsibilities of being married to a man whose all-absorbing purpose in life was to preach the gospel of Jesus Christ, even though the congregation might be small and the financial support inadequate.

An appetite whetted

One positive result of reading Spurgeon's autobiography was an appetite for anything written by the great preacher that I could find. And here I was favoured beyond my wildest imagination. Having been the librarian during the latter part of his studies at Spurgeon's College, Paul had been given duplicates of virtually all Spurgeon's publications. Not only did thirty-one volumes

C. H. Spurgeon's Autobiography.

COMPILED FROM

HIS DIARY, LETTERS, AND RECORDS,

BY

HIS WIFE,

AND HIS PRIVATE SECRETARY.

of *The Sword and the Trowel*[1]
line our shelves but also
copies of nearly forty volumes
of Spurgeon's sermons. But
despite such an abundant
choice, the work that attracted
me the most at this time was
Spurgeon's seven-volume
commentary on the Psalms,
called *The Treasury of David*.
Here was treasure indeed!
Reading a small section each
day, I worked my way through
several of the volumes—which
proved gold dust to my soul.

Psalm 12 was a special
consolation. It begins with two evocative words, 'Help, Lord
…' and Spurgeon says of this prayer, 'A short, sweet, suggestive,

A SERIES OF HOMILETICAL HINTS UPON ALMOST EVERY
VERSE;
AND LISTS OF WRITERS UPON EACH PSALM.

BY

C. H. SPURGEON.

VOL. I.

PSALM I. TO XXVI.

(*Twenty-fourth Thousand.*)

London:
PASSMORE AND ALABASTER, 4, PATERNOSTER BUILDINGS.

1886.

seasonable and serviceable prayer; a kind of angel's sword to be turned every way, and to be used on all occasions.' He then continues,

> '"Help, Lord", is a very useful ejaculation which we may dart up to heaven on occasions of emergency, whether learning, suffering, fighting, living or dying. As small ships can sail into harbours which larger vessels cannot enter, so our brief cries and short petitions may trade with heaven when our soul is wind-bound and business-bound as to longer exercises of devotion and when the stream of grace seems at too low an ebb to float a more laborious supplication.

This was exactly the sort of practical counsel that proved so timely for those early days of motherhood when, deprived of sleep and lacking in anyone besides the redoubtable Dr Benjamin Spock, whose book of advice on childcare was continually at hand, I tried desperately to soothe my crying baby! And, incidentally, this short prayer for help is not just one for new mothers, but is 'serviceable', as Spurgeon says, on many occasions of pressure and anxiety.

The exercise of prayer

I suppose there are no Christians who can honestly say that they find prayer easy. Probably the hardest of all the spiritual exercises, prayer leads into what the apostle Paul describes as the 'heavenly realms' where we not only draw near to God but are also up against the 'powers of this dark world and against the spiritual forces of evil.'[2] As William Cowper so aptly writes:

Restraining prayer, we cease to fight,
Prayer makes the Christian's armour bright;
And Satan trembles when he sees
The weakest saint upon his knees.

It is one of Satan's commonest strategies to keep us from prayer either through tiredness, busyness, or most commonly, a deep sense of unworthiness. Certainly I struggled to pray, often falling asleep on my knees. After the 'heady' days when I had first discovered the writings of Jonathan Edwards and then was introduced to a plethora of notable divines through my marriage, I realized that my head knowledge of Christian experience had far outstripped my heart knowledge. Added to this I recognized to my alarm how self-centred I had been as a single person with no one to worry about except myself. Now with incessant broken nights due to a teething baby and adjustment to married life which was difficult for us both, largely because of my lack of any previous home life, I turned back to a book I had loved as a teenager. It is probably one of the best I know on the subject of prayer—Professor O. Hallesby's book, simply entitled *Prayer*.

Prayer, Hallesby maintains, is for the helpless. 'Prayer and helplessness are inseparable. Only he who is helpless can truly pray.' This was music to my soul. Hallesby continues:

> Listen to this, you who are often so helpless that you do not know what to do. At times you do not even know how to pray. Your mind seems full of sin and impurity … Listen, my friend! Your helplessness is your best prayer. It calls from your heart to the heart of God with greater effect than all your uttered pleas. He hears it from the very moment that you are seized with helplessness and he becomes actively engaged at once in hearing and answering … your wordless prayer. If you are a mother, you will understand this very readily … Your infant child cannot formulate in words a single petition to you. Yet the little one prays the best way he knows how. All he can do is to cry, but you understand very well his pleading cry.

Such words were a great comfort and even though I might literally fall fast asleep while Paul was leading our daily prayer time together, I knew that my Father understood and was leading me gently on in the knowledge of my sins and of his grace.

A love for verse

The arrival of our second child was a delight, and although I now coped better with the demands of a new baby, my reading time also diminished dramatically. Instead my love of verse, kindled in my earliest years of life when my mother used to recite from R. L. Stevenson's *A Child's Garden of Verses* to me at the age of two or three, now resurfaced. Before I left home for my first boarding school at the age of six she introduced me to lines from some of Tennyson's poignant poems. Now, newly married and unable to spend any prolonged time with books, I found lines from some of the great poems of our Christian heritage deeply moving and expressive of desires and emotions I could not easily put into words.

Saint Paul

Perhaps my all-time favourite is F. W. H. Myers' grand poem with the simple title *St Paul*. Whatever Myers' own spiritual position may have been, he caught the heart and vision of the apostle Paul with clarity and tenderness. Consisting of one hundred and forty-five stanzas[3] each four lines in length, he begins with a declaration of Paul's life-statement in Philippians 1:21—'For to me to live is Christ' and 1 Corinthians 2:2 'For I am determined to know nothing among you save Jesus Christ and him crucified':

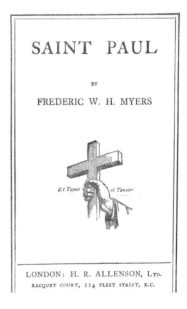

CHRIST, I am Christ's! and let the name suffice you,
Ay, for me too he greatly hath sufficed;
Lo with no winning words I would entice you,
Paul has no honour and no friend but Christ.

The beauty of Christ overwhelms the apostle:

Who that one moment has the least descried him,
Dimly and faintly, hidden and afar,
Doth not despise all excellence beside him,
Pleasures and powers that are not and that are.

But Myers also catches the anguish of Paul's realization that he of all men was the 'chief of sinners'. He had not only consented to Stephen's martyrdom but had himself captured and killed many of the early Christians.

Saints, did I say? With your remembered faces,
Dear men and women whom I sought and slew!
Ah! when we mingle in the heavenly places
How will I weep to Stephen and to you!

He understands the Christian warfare and the struggle believers can so often experience as, despite the battle, sin seems to get the upper hand:

Oh the regret, the struggle and the failing,
Oh the days desolate and useless years!
Vows in the night, so fierce and unavailing!
Stings of my shame and passion of my tears…

Also I ask, but ever from the praying
Shrinks my soul backward, eager and afraid,
Point me the sum and shame of my betraying,
Show me, O Love, the wounds that I have made!
Well, let me sin, but not with my consenting,
Well, let me die, but willing to be whole:

Never, O Christ,—so stay me from relenting—
Shall there be truce betwixt my flesh and soul.

How rightly Myers puts such words as these in the apostle's
mouth as he ends his epic poem:

Yea, thro' life, death, thro' sorrow and thro' sinning
He shall suffice me, for he hath sufficed;
Christ is the end, for Christ was the beginning,
Christ the beginning, for the end is Christ.

By-path Meadow

A knock at the door of our Northallerton Manse alerted us to the arrival of a visitor—an unusual event in those days. It was early in 1964, soon after the birth of our eldest son. Our church treasurer stood on the doorstep, twisting his fingers nervously. 'Mr Cook,' he ventured at last, 'I am sorry to tell you that the church can no longer afford to keep you'—a hard message for that good man to bring. With a membership of little more than fifteen, ten had originally pledged to give a pound a week to support the ministry. We had not been there long before two 'pound-a weekers' were disaffected and left the church.[4] With a pledged offering dropping to eight pounds a week and some help from the Baptist Union Home Work fund, we knew that the situation was dire. Clearly that struggling northern church, built on a new estate outside the main town, could not afford to maintain the church building, the ministry, the manse and support our growing family.

A settled home

Reluctantly, for Paul had a keen awareness of the needs of the North of England, we prepared to leave and were grateful for a call to serve a church in a small town in the Midlands. Shepshed, once a hamlet figuring in the Domesday Book of 1086 as Scepeshefde Regis, had adopted its present name in 1888. Now in 1964 it had a population of about 6,000[5] and presented an excellent challenge in comparison with our bleak northern situation.

To me, the spacious manse, with an extensive garden containing a small orchard of fruit trees, soft fruit bushes of many varieties, and even more significantly a kindly church membership, represented a sort of earthly paradise. Shepshed was God's gift to me, a settled home after my turbulent childhood years in north-west China, followed by a boarding school education and difficult early years of marriage due largely to my total lack of early home life. Then came the abrupt closure to the ministry in Northallerton after little more than three years.

However, spiritually it also presented some of the characteristics of By-path Meadow pictured in John Bunyan's *The Pilgrim's Progress*. In that allegory this path, leading through luscious meadow land, represented ease and comfort after the sorrows of Vanity Fair where Faithful had been martyred and the road the pilgrims had just been following was 'rough and their feet [made] tender by reason of their travels.'

The birth of two more sons in fairly quick succession brought the family to four in number; our daughter, Esther, now had three brothers—all four under the age of seven. It also brought considerable problems to their somewhat impractical mother and a steep learning curve in household management! Reading time in those pressurized days was clearly at a severe premium.

Looking back over the regular weekly letters I wrote to my parents in Malaysia, I discover many details of family life that I would have forgotten. My father, Stanley Rowe, was one of life's natural hoarders and he kept every letter I had written to them from a child of thirteen until he and my mother eventually came back to England in 1976. These he presented to me, all stuffed into two shoe boxes.

Spiritual obstacles

As a family during the early years of marriage we faced continual ill health. Not only did the children suffer all the usual childhood ailments, but it seemed that constant stomach germs laid everyone low, infections passing rapidly through the family. Not only were the children poorly, but Paul himself experienced recurrent illness. As a bride of twenty-three, I had little understood the significance of my promises of support 'in sickness and in health,' and it seemed that the former would certainly dominate our marriage as I was soon to learn. More seriously, such constant illness meant that my attendance at services of worship on Sundays was spasmodic at best. At times I find from my letters that ten weeks could elapse without me being able to be present at a service due to family illness. Even when I was able to attend, the care of a row of small boys was not conducive to easy listening as any parent will know.

Without doubt these years proved a 'By-path Meadow' to my soul. I rested in the security of past blessings with which I had certainly been favoured and maintained the outward forms of prayer and the reading of Scripture, yet my heart was not in it. Often lacking in sleep, I took refuge in the fact that the Lord understood the situation and so made little attempt to fight the spiritual lethargy I was experiencing. But the great Shepherd of the sheep is well able to seek out any of his flock that are wandering in a wilderness, and this he did, and once again it was by means of a book.

A challenging holiday

We were on holiday in a remote Welsh valley in 1971. Certainly the advertisement we had answered made the choice of this self-catering cottage look idyllic. In days when standards were much lower than today, our first shock was to discover that only a flimsy gate stood between the garden and the fast-moving traffic on the adjacent road. With an adventurous toddler who could well open gates, this was troubling. The furnishings were shabby with large holes in the reupholstered covers of the three-piece suite. But worst of all was the setting on the electricity meter. Fed by shilling coins, we quickly discovered that our coins were 'eaten up' in moments, making any cooked meals prohibitive. Even to boil a kettle was costly, and to bath the children, out of the question.

The Heavenly Footman

With this setting, it was an anxious few days, not made any easier when Paul announced that he must drive all the way home to attend a farewell service for one of our students. I was left alone in a highly unsatisfactory environment with the entire responsibility for a lively family aged between two and nine. With the children settled in bed one night, I sat on the tattered settee and idly picked up a book we had brought with us for holiday reading.

Bearing the quaint title *The Heavenly Footman*, it was by John Bunyan.[6] Only forty-eight pages in length and in large print, I assumed it would be quick and easy to read. Never had I been more mistaken and shaken by what I read. Addressed to 'All Slothful and Careless People', Bunyan's first shaft hit hard.

What shall I say? Time runs; and will you be slothful? Much of your lives are past; and will you be slothful? Your souls are worth a thousand worlds; and will you be slothful? The day of death and judgment is at the door; and will you be slothful? The curse of God hangs over your heads; and will you be slothful? Besides the devils are earnest, laborious, and seek by all means every day, by every sin, to keep you out of heaven … and will you be slothful?

I was riveted and afraid, and that was just the introduction. I turned the bulky pages and discovered that Bunyan's text was derived from 1 Corinthians 9:24, 'So run that you may obtain' [the prize].

Written in block capitals throughout the book was Bunyan's own rendering of that verse: THEY THAT WILL HAVE HEAVEN MUST RUN FOR IT. Was I running for heaven? The answer was sadly, 'No'. Maybe I was ambling, but certainly not running. He further defined 'running' as 'FLYING' (i.e. running at top speed) and then 'PRESSING' and lastly 'CONTINUING.' I fell at each hurdle except possibly the last. This certainly was not comforting bedtime reading.

By page four I was thoroughly alarmed. Bunyan continues: 'There are many that do run, yea, and run far

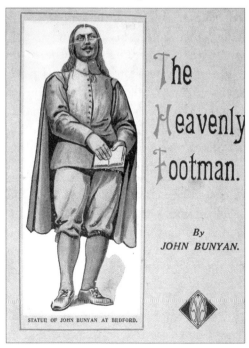

The Heavenly Footman.

By
JOHN BUNYAN.

STATUE OF JOHN BUNYAN AT BEDFORD.

too, who yet miss of the crown that standeth at the end of the race ... You know that all that do run in a race do not obtain the victory ... What! do you think that every heavy-heeled professor will have heaven? What! every lazy one?' A page or two later Bunyan issues a further dire warning: 'If thou lose, thou losest all, thou losest soul, God, Christ, heaven, ease, peace, etc.'

A timely warning

Of course I knew the clear biblical teaching of Christian perseverance; that true believers, though they may struggle and backslide are not abandoned, and that Christ has promised that 'None shall pluck them out of my hand.' But the warning was timely. I already knew of some of my contemporaries who had abandoned their early professions of faith. Yet Bunyan had a true pastoral heart as he gives instructions on 'How to run.' 'Cry to God,' he tells the troubled believer, 'that he would inflame thy will ... with the things of the other world.' He gives an example of Jacob at the Brook Jabbok when he wrestled with the Angel of the Lord. 'I will not let thee go except thou bless me.' 'I WILL, I WILL, I WILL! O this blessed inflamed will for heaven.' Bunyan continues by giving 'the saints of old' as examples of perseverance. 'What could stop them? Could fire or faggot, sword, stinking dungeons, whips, bears, bulls, lions, cruel rackings, stoning, starving, nakedness?' Obviously I had no excuses.

By this time, I was conscious of little else except my need to run for heaven with all the diligence I could muster and was ready for Bunyan's words of consolation: 'To encourage thee a little farther, set to the work, and when thou hast run thyself down weary, then the Lord Jesus will take thee up and carry thee. Is this not enough to make any poor soul begin his race?'[7]

As on many occasions of deep emotional significance in our lives, we can remember small details with vivid clarity, and as

I knelt at that tatty settee, after finishing the book, I can even remember distinctly the shape of the holes in the covers as with many tears I prayed the words of a well-known hymn:

> O Jesus, I have promised
> To serve thee to the end;
> Be thou for ever near me,
> My Master and my Friend.
> I shall not fear the battle,
> If thou art by my side,
> Nor wander from the pathway,
> If thou wilt be my guide.

And added with all the sincerity I could summon:

> O give me grace to follow,
> My Master and my Friend.

The power of hymns

*T*he years that followed were routine: joyful, sad, hectic, troubling and distressing in turns. The birth of a fourth son, the cheerful and imperturbable Edward, added to the family mix and the boys became a staunch unit—a cricket team, a football team or whatever else took their interest. Yes, most certainly there were fights and tensions but loyalty was paramount.

During 1971 we had moved from the manse of the Shepshed Baptist church owing to a sad division in the original church. This was largely on doctrinal grounds, but one unforeseen consequence was that now, with the help of a friend, we had been able to buy our own home. A beautiful four bedroomed house, with a handsome fitted kitchen was a luxury for those days. Complete with a large weeping willow in the front garden, a tree that our eldest son Jerry used to climb with great delight and remain entirely hidden in its branches, it was an ideal setting—a gift from our heavenly Father.

This home, together with the newly formed congregation that had come into being as a result of the split, was the backdrop for some of the most useful years of Paul's ministry. With growing numbers and several significant conversions, they were encouraging times. In our new home we were privileged with visits from many fine Christian men, mainly coming to us as visiting preachers for the church. The reward of entertaining such men far outweighed any extra work it might entail. As each of the bedrooms was occupied by the family, one being used as Paul's study, our four boys sleeping in another in bunk beds and two single beds, and Esther with a small bedroom to herself, our guests usually slept on the bed settee in the front room—a long bright red settee. The thought of how many animated conversations had been conducted late into the night on that very settee before our guests could sleep on it, made me reluctant to part with it, when it eventually wore out.

Christian Hymns

In this home too the first edition of *Christian Hymns* had its birth. I served numerous cups of coffee and chocolate biscuits to Paul and his fellow editor, Graham Harrison, as they toiled for long hours, compiling the hymns, checking on dates and versions and arranging them for that first stubby little red hymn book with its two trumpeters in one corner of the cover. It was published in 1978 at a time when a new hymn book was sorely needed in the churches and is still used by many congregations even today.

Some of the hymns introduced into that book hold very special memories. One evening in June 1978 as we listened to the six o'clock news we heard of a grievous massacre of Western missionaries—staff at an Elim Pentecostal school in present day Zimbabwe. We listened as the names of the missionaries—three men, six women and four children were slowly read out. We gasped with horror as we heard the last name of the list—Wendy White, a dear friend of ours. Brutally bayoneted to death, their bodies mutilated almost beyond recognition, thrown into the bush and abandoned, Wendy's death and that of her fellow missionaries left us reeling. As she died Wendy had called out, 'Fear not those who kill the body—they cannot kill the soul.' That night we stood together round the piano and sang a new hymn introduced into that hymn book:

> From heavenly Jerusalem's towers
> The path through the desert they trace;
> And every affliction they suffered,
> Redounds to the glory of grace.
> Their look they cast back on the tempests,
> On fears, on grim death and the grave,
> Rejoicing that now they're in safety,
> Through him that is mighty to save.[8]

That same hymn was sung at the funeral of Doctor Martyn Lloyd-Jones in 1981, a preacher whom we loved and had been honoured to entertain in our home.

Another hymn became very precious to me personally in those days. Perhaps the language is a little dated to modern ears, but its words never fail to move me still:

> Jesus, priceless treasure,
> Source of purest pleasure,
> Truest friend to me!
> Ah! How long I've panted,
> And my heart has fainted,
> Thirsting Lord for thee!
> Thine I am, O spotless Lamb,
> I will suffer naught to hide thee,
> Naught I ask beside thee.[9]

Wesley's Hymns

The book contained even more of Charles Wesley's magnificent hymns than the newer Methodist hymn books have done and words such as these expressed my own longings, especially in days when the cares of a growing family seemed overwhelming:

> O that I might for ever sit
> With Mary at the Master's feet,
> Be this my happy choice:
> My only care, delight and bliss,
> My joy, my heaven on earth be this—
> To hear the Bridegroom's voice!

In another moving hymn expressing penitence yet confidence in the blood of Jesus to cleanse and renew, Wesley begins with the words:

> Depth of mercy, can there be,
> Mercy still reserved for me?
> Can my God his wrath forbear?
> Me, the chief of sinners, spare?

And then he answers his own question:

> There for me the Saviour stands;
> Shows his wounds and spreads his hands.
> God is love, I know, I feel;
> Jesus lives and loves me still.

Surprising as it may seem, the twelve verses of Wesley's magnificent devotional poem, based on the story of the patriarch Jacob wrestling with the Angel, all find a place in *Christian Hymns*. A shortened six verse version is also included, possibly suitable for singing as a hymn. As Jacob struggles to discover the name of his unknown opponent and to overcome him, he cries out:

I need not tell thee who I am,
My misery and sin declare …
But who I ask thee, who art thou?
Tell me thy name and tell me now.

He is determined to prevail against his antagonist whom he now realizes is no ordinary foe:

In vain thou strugglest to get free;
I never will unloose my hold!
Art thou the Man that died for me?
The secret of thy love unfold.
Wrestling I will not let thee go,
Till I thy name, thy nature know.

And as he finally receives the longed-for blessing from the Angel, whom he now recognizes as a manifestation the pre-incarnate Christ, he exclaims:

I know thee, Saviour, who thou art,
Jesus, the feeble sinner's friend;
Nor wilt thou with the night depart,
But stay and love me to the end.
Thy mercies never shall remove:
Thy nature and thy name is Love

Isaac Watts once said that he rated that one hymn of Charles Wesley's above all the hymns and poems that he himself had written.

William Williams

Also introduced into *Christian Hymns* were some of the most beautiful lines by the Welsh poet William Williams, known as the Poet of the Revival. Williams' hymns are packed with theology, yet deeply experimental. Many of his lines would suddenly spring into his mind in the middle of the night. Well-prepared, he went to bed with pen and ink, complete with a board on which to rest his paper. Perhaps the following words had their genesis during one sleepless night:

> Jesus, Jesus, all-sufficient,
> Beyond telling is thy worth;
> In thy name lie greater treasures
> Than the riches found on earth.
> Such abundance,
> Is my portion with my God.
>
> In thy gracious face there's beauty,
> Far surpassing every thing
> Found in all the earth's great wonders
> Mortal eye hath ever seen.
> Rose of Sharon,
> Thou thyself art heaven's delight.[10]

It would be hard to find in the whole of hymnody lines of more depth and passionate longing for the presence of Christ that these by William Williams:

> Dear Jesus, come, my soul doth groan
> For naught but for thyself alone,
> Thou art the pearl of price;
> For thee I'd part with all below,
> And every hardship undergo
> Beneath the vaulted skies.
>
> Thy presence can without delay,
> Drive all my numerous cares away
> As chaff before the wind;
> Compose my soul to adore and love
> Thee as an object far above,
> To thee alone inclined.

James Montgomery

Another poet whose work can be ranked among the finest in hymnody was James Montgomery (1771–1854). From his boyhood Montgomery had aspirations to be a great poet, but he was the despair of his Moravian school masters who wished him to follow his parents into the Moravian ministry. Much of the poetry which he wrote in later life has been forgotten, but his hymns live on, and one I found deeply moving was a two-verse hymn that is placed in the section of the hymn book on the Lord's Supper, but seems to me more suitable for personal meditation of the cross:

> When on Calvary I rest,
> God in the flesh made manifest
> Shines in my Redeemer's face,
> Full of beauty, truth and grace.
>
> Here I would for ever stay,
> Weep and gaze my soul away;
> Thou art heaven on earth to me,
> Lovely, mournful Calvary.

Charlotte Elliott

The intercession of Christ for his needy broken people is the theme of another hymn introduced into the book—a little-known composition of Charlotte Elliott's. An invalid much of her life, Charlotte experienced periods of depression and loneliness, but out of her sufferings came some of her finest hymns. These lines had especial significance for me at times when I became most acutely aware of sin and failure:

> O thou, the contrite sinner's friend,
> Who loving, lovest to the end,

On this alone my hopes depend,
That thou wilt plead for me.

When Satan by my sins made bold,
Strives from the cross to loose my hold,
Then with thy pitying arms enfold,
And plead, O plead for me.

Modern hymns

The book also included some 'modern' hymns—certainly modern by 1970s standards. When Bishop Timothy Dudley-Smith first published his great hymn—a hymn that has now become a classic—*Tell out my soul, the greatness of the Lord* in the *Anglican Hymn Book* in 1965, it instantly became a favourite, and was included in *Christian Hymns.* Vernon Higham's warmly devotional hymns also found a place in the new book with *I saw a new vision of Jesus* becoming a favourite. Written while the author was seriously ill in hospital, lines such as these become more meaningful and poignant:

For yonder a light shines eternal,
Which spreads through the valley of gloom
Lord Jesus, resplendent and regal,
Drives fear far away from the tomb.
Our God is the end of the journey,
His pleasant and glorious domain,
For there are the children of mercy,
Who praise him for Calvary's pain.

A few of the editors' own hymns also found a place in the new book. Graham Harrison's rendering of Psalm 130 has a pathos that accurately reflects the cry of the Psalmist:

Out of the depths I cry to thee,
Lord, hear me, I implore thee;

If thou should'st mark iniquity,
Who, Lord, should stand before thee?
O may thine ear attend my cry!
Lord, bid me to thyself draw nigh,
While now I call upon thee.

When Paul was preparing a sermon based on the praises of heaven for the 'Lamb who was slain' in Revelation 5, he could not find any hymn that satisfactorily echoed the thoughts he wished to express. So he scribbled down some lines of his own—accomplished from start to finish as he tells me in about twenty minutes. Coming down to the kitchen he read the words to me—an enormous surprise as he had never done anything of the sort before. The hymn, coupled with an excellent tune, has gained popularity in many circles.

Rise with me—my soul in triumph,
Mounts to see the Prince of kings;
Draw with me the flood which issues
From the boundless heavenly springs.
There together let us wonder,
Gaze upon the Lamb that died;
Bow before the Victor reigning
Glory in the flowing tide.

Time would certainly 'fail me to tell of' all the excellent new hymns that found a place in *Christian Hymns* (edition 1)[11]—and perhaps my readers are glad of that. But one simple hymn written by Annie Johnson Flint, has certainly brought much consolation to those using the book as it gives promise of the abundant grace of God that is more than sufficient for every need. Based on James 4:6 she writes:

He giveth more grace when the burden grows greater.
He sendeth more strength when the labours increase;

To added affliction, he addeth his mercy,
To multiplied trials, his multiplied peace.

His love has no limit, his grace has no measure,
His power has no boundary known unto men;
For out of his infinite riches in Jesus
He giveth, and giveth, and giveth again!

When we have exhausted our store of endurance,
When our strength has failed ere the day is half done,
When we reach the end of our hoarded resources,
Our Father's full giving is only begun.

An unforgettable night

*A*nd then I began to read! Yes, again! With Esther now sixteen and our youngest, Edward, turning five and at school, I suddenly opened my eyes once more to the treasure trove of books all around me in our home. For years the care of the family had meant that reading time was strictly limited—in fact had almost vanished.

Other interests had crowded in, not least the rearing, breeding and exhibiting of a very attractive variety of Dutch rabbits. I sold young rabbits whose markings did not reach the standard for exhibition to the pet shops, but soon realized, good though my stock was, I could not compete with the professionals. As I stood among these top class breeders, each waiting proudly beside his exhibit, cigarette hanging on his bottom lip, I felt oddly out of place! When my best exhibit only received a second prize at a

Leicester show I gradually began to recognize that this absorbing interest was robbing me of far greater concerns and indeed of spiritual zeal itself.

An altered perspective

Then God intervened again. The night of 26 November 1978 was one that I now regard as the most significant catalyst in my entire spiritual life. Nothing outwardly dramatic happened, but everything changed. During the July of that year I had heard a sermon preached by the elder of our church on Psalm 30:5—'Weeping may endure for a night, but joy comes in the morning.' It was a message that sprang out of the preacher's own personal suffering. The theme was that life in this broken, evil and sorrowing world holds many tears, whether we are Christians or not. But for the believer a morning of joy will dawn—a morning of pure unclouded joy in heaven. Foretastes of that joy may well be ours in this life, but unending delight awaits us on the New Earth with Christ. The preacher pointed out that the verse contains both a limitation and a certainty. Weeping is *only* for a night, but the morning of joy will last forever. I had already known much weeping in my life: the death of my two young brothers, one in particularly tragic circumstances, the loss of parental care during my childhood and teenage years, the death of my close friend Shirley Paget-Wilkes in a drowning accident and more recently the grievous death of Wendy White, together with the ups and downs of home and church life. I thought much about that message, but as the months passed its significance grew on me, until at last I plucked up courage to ask the preacher for a copy of his notes.

That November night was a night of nights to me. For some reason, I cannot remember why, I was sleeping on the red settee in the front room, and before settling for the night read through the notes. The result took me totally by surprise. Sleep was forgotten as I was given an experience of God's power and presence that was quite unforgettable. I saw in a flash that I had expected, even felt I *deserved*, a measure of joy in this life and deeply resented the sorrows I had known. I realized at last that true undying joy awaits me 'in the morning'—in heaven. Yes, there are many joys remaining while here on earth, but these, I now saw, come as a bonus not as my right: the beauty of young spring leaves, the gasp of surprise at some act of unexpected kindness, a robin on my bird table, the warmth of a little child's hand in mine—these and many, many more that we may know here and now are all bonuses of joy.

This may seem insignificant to my reader, but it altered my entire perspective, changing my expectations of life as I knew it and setting my hopes on the eternal city. Life itself did not change. I still had four boys to care for and hustle off to school in the morning, sort out and pair up dozens of socks, iron Paul's shirts, not to mention cleaning out endless rabbit hutches. But everything had changed. For six weeks or more it seemed that nothing could mar my joy. Of course this did not last, but my changed attitudes did.

Everlasting Rest

I began to ferret out books on heaven to feed my new longings. But, aware of the temptation to be a mere escapist, I needed to clarify my thinking. A glass-fronted bookcase that stood in our front room under lock and key especially attracted me. It contained Paul's most valuable books, many of them works from the Puritan era spanning the sixteenth and seventeenth centuries. I opened the book case with care and began to scan the titles. Then I spotted one that answered my quest: *The Saints' Everlasting Rest,* by Richard Baxter—a handsome volume despite its broken back.

The chapter headings gave me a quick overview of Baxter's teaching, shaped by his own intense sufferings. Born in 1615, Baxter had exercised a memorable ministry in Kidderminster before being ejected from his church by the 1662 Act of Uniformity. In that dark year two thousand other pastors and teachers were also expelled from their churches because their consciences would not allow them to conform to words and practices introduced into the revised *Book of Common Prayer.* Facing constant arrest, in and out of prison, Baxter also experienced multiple periods of illness, the early death of his well-loved wife Margaret and his own final cruel trial and imprisonment under the notorious and coarse Judge George Jeffreys. Baxter was then an emaciated old man of seventy, but Jeffreys wished to see the preacher flogged through the streets of London. Certainly Baxter knew what he was talking about!

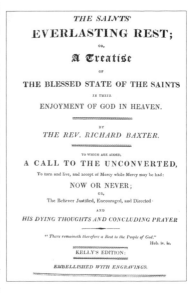

Such headings as *The Saints' Rest is not to be expected on earth* and *Directions how to live a heavenly life on earth*, chimed with my own thinking at this time. But it was Baxter's final chapter, *Heavenly Contemplation Exemplified* that grabbed my attention. Baxter gives numerous examples of how to meditate on heaven, an exercise which is notoriously difficult as we are lifted into a realm largely hidden from us. No one, Baxter insists, would think of buying a house without looking round it carefully first. The believer should 'visit' heaven often in imagination, he maintained. This was a new dimension for me and I copied out long passages into a notebook I had started keeping. The language was certainly quaint, but after reading it through a number of times, I began to grasp Baxter's meaning:

O my soul, look above this world of sorrows. Hast thou so long felt the smarting rod of affliction, and no better understood its meaning? Is not every stroke to drive thee hence?

Ah, my dear Lord, I feel thy meaning … my heart thou aimest at, thy rod drives, thy silken cord of love draws and all to bring it to thyself. Lord, can such a heart be worth thou having? Make it worthy, and then it is thine, take it to thyself and then take me …

Heavenly longing

One reaction to my new perspective on life did indeed become an inordinate longing for 'the heavenly country'. Philippians 1:23 became a favourite verse. With the Apostle Paul I too could say that I had a 'desire to depart and be with Christ which is far better.' It little occurred to me in those heady days that God might have further work for me to do on this earth and anyway I had five children and a husband (not to mention elderly parents now retired and living nearby) who might need my care. To balance these two factors was all-important. And once again Richard Baxter expressed a vital corrective to my thinking. He, more than most, had good cause to say:

> Thou knowest I am not weary of thy work, but of sorrow and sin. I am willing to stay while thou wilt employ me … but I beseech thee, [let me] stay no longer when this is done, and while I must be here, let me be still amending and still ascending; make me still better and take me at the best. I dare not be so impatient as to importune thee to cut off my time, and snatch me hence unready, because I know that my everlasting state so much depends on the improvement of this life. Nor would I stay when my work is done, and remain here sinning while my brethren are triumphing.

In a new spirit of meekness I now prayed with this saint of old:

> Lord, I am content to stay thy time, and go thy way, so thou wilt

exalt me also in thy season, and take me into thy barn when thou seest me ripe.

The Glory of Heaven

With the sweeping changes that have taken place in the English language in recent years, many of today's readers may well find such writings too quaint and inaccessible to be of much benefit. However a modern work by John F. MacArthur is a superb alternative. The title in itself is comprehensive: *The Glory of Heaven: the truth about heaven, angels and eternal life.* A magnificent compendium on the life to come, the chapter titles are also evocative: *No earthly idea about heaven* is one such, and another, equally compelling, is headed, *What we will be like in heaven?* Added to the main bulk of his book, MacArthur provides four long appraisals that deal with the thoughts on the subject by Richard Baxter, Thomas Boston, C. H. Spurgeon and J C Ryle, a period covering the seventeenth century onwards.

Concluding one chapter, MacArthur touches the longings and conflicts of all believers:

> Although sin has crippled our souls and marred our spirits— though it has scarred our thoughts, wills and emotions—we who know Christ have already had a taste of what redemption is like. And so we long for that day when we will be completely redeemed. We yearn to reach that place where the seed of perfection that has been planted within us will bloom into fullness and we will be completely redeemed, finally made perfect. That is exactly what heaven is about.[12]

A night of weeping

*H*ow often it is true that a period of unusual blessing is followed by a time of sorrow or trial. Undoubtedly the former is God's merciful preparation to strengthen his people when the coming trouble may seem too hard to bear. Such trials can come in a multitude of ways as any conversation with another Christian will quickly testify. But in our case the pain and difficulties arose mainly in the area of our home life.

It is probable that in most homes and marriages there are periods of particular strain and tension. And this is especially so in the lives of a pastor and his wife. Satan, our arch enemy, is ever out to destroy a preacher who is seeing days of spiritual usefulness in his ministry. My husband Paul had been experiencing many years of intense pressure, preaching fresh sermons two or three times a week, travelling all over the country to various church functions, writing articles, giving lectures, preparing and editing *Christian Hymns*, and guiding an infant church. So it is not surprising that his nervous health began to give way. In addition, the burden of a large and active family had not been an easy one for him, nor had he taken any regular days off for relaxation for many years, as far as I can recollect.

Sanctifying purposes

It may well be that I lacked a clear understanding of the depths of Paul's need and was less than helpful at such a time. The strains we experienced were compounded by the enormous difference between our personalities and backgrounds. When Paul asked me to marry him he had no idea of my irregular childhood and upbringing, nor had I appreciated his more traditional one. Paul's father worked in the civil service: a wise, judicious and careful man who watched over his family diligently. His mother was a kind, loving, if over-anxious person. The home was therefore well regulated and orderly, the children nurtured in correct protocol.

My early childhood, on the other hand, was spent in the wilds of north-west China, where rats infested the premises and toilets were merely large open-air pits. My father was a dedicated pioneer missionary whose work always took prior place in his life to other concerns, while his adventurous spirit could often lead him to take enormous risks with his young family. After the age of six I was sent to boarding schools often in hazardous situations and from then on to institutions of various sorts with no further home life. As a result of these differences Paul was disciplined and orderly, with high expectations—expectations that my far-less-orderly mind and lack of home background found hard to achieve. Nevertheless, such differences were clearly in God's sanctifying purposes for us both. But certainly the few years following 1978 were a 'night of weeping' in our experience.

When God's children suffer

Before long it became evident that Paul's nervous health had deteriorated to such an extent that he was no longer able to continue with the ministry. It was an experimental period medically and the drugs which Paul was prescribed have long since been banned as seriously detrimental to overall health. This situation obviously brought enormous pressure on me; not only was I trying to cope with Paul's illness but was also struggling to hold the family together and keep the boys quiet when Paul was needing rest. It could certainly be described as 'a night of weeping.'

When the first child of Horatius Bonar, the Scottish hymn writer, and his wife Jane, died at a year old, Bonar wrote one of his early titles, called simply *Night of Weeping*—a book offering an interpretation of suffering in the lives of believers. Now published under the title *When God's children suffer*,[13] it has brought consolation to many troubled Christians passing through often inexplicable sorrows. Suffering, says Bonar, (and he well knew what that meant, for he and his wife would lose five of their young children over the years), is the family badge of all true believers as they follow Christ, the Man of Sorrows. Describing the spiritual benefits reaped from days of suffering, Bonar says, 'In eternity we shall praise Jehovah most of all for our sorrows and tears ... We shall then know how utterly unworthy we were of all his grace ... Our joys were all of grace—pure grace—much more our sorrows. It is out of the "exceeding riches of God's grace" that trial comes.' Pure spiritual gain often springs from suffering.

Thomas Boston

In addition to Bonar's beautiful and helpful book, I came across another old volume on Paul's bookshelves: the *Memoirs of Thomas Boston of Ettrick*—a book that put my own problems into perspective. Its old-fashioned style was quite a barrier at first, particularly when Boston starts off by telling us that in 1676 he was 'procreated betwixt John Boston and Alison Trotter, a woman prudent and virtuous.' But as I read on I discovered in Boston, an earlier Scottish preacher, a man of astounding ability, godliness and self-denial, and one who bore his many sufferings with a patience that amazed me. However dark the providences of his life, his trust in God never wavered.

When Thomas Boston met Catherine Brown in 1697 it was a case of love at first sight. As he expressed it, 'something stuck with me', and clearly 'stuck' permanently for they married soon afterwards. He almost exhausts vocabulary as he searches out words in praise of Catherine. She was:

> ... a woman of great worth, whom I therefore passionately loved, and inwardly honoured: a stately, beautiful personage, truly pious ... patient in our common tribulations ... a woman of bright natural parts ... of quick and lively apprehension, great presence of mind, sagacious and acute in discerning the qualities of persons, modest and grave, but naturally cheerful ... a crown to me in my public appearances.

Boston is largely remembered today for his doctrinal work *Human Nature in its Fourfold State* and in what was known as the *Marrow Controversy*. In this doctrinal dispute he strongly defended the scriptural teaching of free grace by which a sinner may cast himself on Christ for forgiveness and mercy without any preconditions. This was in opposition to those of the Scottish presbytery who held a legalistic teaching that demanded a certain standard of life and achievement before a sinner was qualified to believe and be accepted into God's family. Boston's position can be summed up in words later written by Charlotte Elliot:

> Just as I am and waiting not
> To rid my soul of one dark blot

To thee whose blood can cleanse each spot,
O Lamb of God, I come.

The Crook in the Lot

Although his life story challenged me, it was in a small work called
The Crook in the Lot, published after Boston's death, that I found
the greatest help—a work occasioned by the sufferings he and his
beautiful wife Catherine had endured together. Of the ten children
Catherine had borne, six had died in
infancy, some in particularly sad
circumstances. With her own
physical health already frail from the
effects of difficult confinements and
multiplied sorrows, a yet more
grievous condition developed when
Catherine was just forty-seven. She
began to suffer with a complaint
which we today would call a form of
dementia. Intermittent at first, her
condition gradually deteriorated.
Occasionally the dark clouds would
roll back and her lovely personality
coupled with her strong faith would

shine out once more. But these occasions grew less and less
frequent until Thomas could describe his Catherine as being 'free
among the dead.' Despite his earnest prayers no clear deliverance
was granted, and at length Boston could only call their shared
sorrows, 'a crook in the lot'—a reference to Ecclesiastes 7:13.

A 'crook in the lot' in Boston's definition is some form of
suffering which God in his sovereign purposes allows into our
lives—circumstances which mar our joys and seem to us to be
totally unexplained and without obvious remedy. A 'crook' is

not a passing situation like a short-lived illness which is soon to be followed by renewed health. Our lives, as we know, are composed of numerous strands: parents, homes, upbringing, health, education, abilities, marriage, employment and many more. Most of these strands, Boston suggests, will run horizontally following a more-or-less straight line, but in the experiences of many there will be 'a crook in the lot'—a single strand that runs contrary to all the others and causes constant distress. These 'crooks' may be removed in this life when God determines, and particularly when we humbly submit to his ways. But very often they will only be straightened out in the life to come and are purposed by God to keep us trusting in him and clinging to him for grace and strength to cope.

Because we live in a broken and fallen world we cannot avoid seeing these 'crooks' both in our own lives and in those of our friends. But Boston explains that such circumstances are allowed by God for our good. With many biblical examples, such as Hannah's infertility, Joseph's imprisonment, Job's manifold trials, Paul's 'thorn in the flesh', he reinforces his point. God may allow a 'crook' to convict us of sin, to bring us back to himself when we stray from him, or to keep us depending on him.

A remedy for 'crooks'

Is there then no remedy for the 'crooks' that mar our lives? Certainly there is. 'There is no crook but what may be remedied by God and made perfectly straight,' Boston maintains. Quoting such promises as 'Call on me in the day of trouble and I will deliver you and you will glorify me,' he points out that God allows such things in our lives order to humble us, to bring us to himself in prayer and to show his glory. When the purpose for the 'crook' is accomplished, God may well 'straighten' it out. Prayer itself, he continues, can be a by-product of our 'crook' and bring us into new communion with God. For almost a hundred and fifty pages of closely-packed argument Boston deals with this subject of trials for the Christian in a sensitive and helpful way.

But what if, like Boston himself in the case of his beloved Catherine, there is no easing of the 'crook' in this life? Some burdens must be carried to the grave. It reminds me of my own mother. When she was dying someone referred to the loss of her two little boys, one as a baby and one in a tragic road accident. He read a passage of Scripture to her that speaks of 'our light affliction which is but for a moment'. Turning her face to the wall in her hospital bed, she said, 'But it wasn't a light affliction.' No, it wasn't, and it was a grief she hardly ever spoke of but carried in silence much of her long life. Yet Boston consoles us by quoting Job 22:29 in the KJV, 'There is lifting up', if not in time, certainly in eternity for the believer.

In conclusion he assures us, 'Though God's humbled children may both breakfast and dine on the bread of adversity and water of affliction, they will be sure to sup sweetly and plentifully.' Heaven will make amends for it all.

Invest your suffering

Among the best recent books on the subject of a believer's sufferings must rank Paul Mallard's title, *Invest your suffering—unexpected intimacy with a loving God*. With painful honesty Mallard describes the long-term illness of his wife Edrie. 'I have struggled,' he tells us, 'with seeing my wife stripped of her dignity and reduced by her agony. I have doubted all kinds of things. I have exploded and lashed out … Chronic illness never goes away.' And yet, despite such circumstances, Paul Mallard can still say that as a result of such suffering, :

> The first thing that happened was that my fellowship with God

was deeper and more intense than it had ever been before. Suffering is the best commentary on God's character and pain is the fittest exposition of his excellences. We discover more about God's grace when we come to the end of ourselves. You will never know that God is all you need until God is all you have got.[14]

As I myself look back on the tumultuous four years when Paul was far from well, I can add a resolute 'Amen' to those words. God taught me much during that time which I could have learnt in no other way.

The printed page—my pastor

*A*ny study of revivals in the life of the church of Jesus Christ makes us quickly aware that God has his own 'times and seasons' when he pours out his blessings on his people in an unusual degree. The apostle Peter refers to such periods as 'times of refreshing from the presence of the Lord' when the church is privileged to know revived spiritual life and unexpected conversions often to a high and wonderful extent.

But there are other occasions when God seems to draw particularly near to his people, maybe not in the full blessings of revival as it has normally been described, but in significant and often surprising awareness of spiritual things, of his holiness and of his presence. He gives an enabling to speak to others who have shown little or no previous concern about eternal things. Unusual answers to prayer and conversions often take place at such times as a new spirit of prayer is felt among Christian people, both in personal prayer and in the church prayer meetings. I have heard from a number of different sources and churches in far separate locations that such a period of spiritual quickening was experienced by many Christians both individually and in their churches during the period 1978–1982. It was most certainly true in the East Midlands. One preacher from Wales who had known such times many years ago in his own ministry commented on 'a sense of God' that he experienced when he visited the area.

Times for extraordinary prayer

Aware of God's nearness, I felt the need to experience much more effectiveness in prayer. I reached down our enormous copy of William Gurnall's commentary on Ephesians 6, *The Christian in Complete Armour* and flicked my way through until I reached his comments on verse 18, 'praying at all times in the Spirit with all prayer and supplication …' After pointing out all the hindrances that Satan throws in the way of personal and corporate prayer, I noted that Gurnall urges believers to extra and intense prayer at those times when God seemed willing to bless his people in a new way. Despite his quaint seventeenth century language, Gurnall's point is clear:[15]

> Times of great expectation are times for extraordinary prayer …
> as the cocks crow thickest towards the break of day, so the saints,
> the nearer they have apprehended the accomplishment of promises
> made to his church the more instant they used to be in prayer.[16]

But how could I, with five children to care for, and a husband far from well, give myself to the sort of urgent prayer that this past preacher was calling for? So often, however, God gives what he requires of us and during these years, years of frequent heartache, I found I actually wanted to pray more than I had ever done before. To help me I turned back to a previous source of encouragement:

the writings of C. H. Spurgeon. And here I found abundant instruction and stimulation on the subject of prayer. Once again the printed page had become my pastor.

The key to the treasure chest

With an almost-complete collection of Spurgeon's sermons lining our bookshelves, I had in my hand the key to an amazing treasure chest. I turned to the index of the sermons and found the ones that dealt specifically with the subject of prayer. I read and reread many passages, and copied out sections which struck me as particularly helpful. Spurgeon was a kindly teacher, taking his hearers on from simple basic principles to some of the most profound concepts that I have ever read on the subject of prayer.

Sermons preached during the year 1860 were particularly significant. The great revivals of 1859 that had swept through America, and on into Wales, Scotland and many parts of England had stirred up Christians to pray urgently for yet greater blessings, and Spurgeon addressed the subject of prayer constantly during this year. Sermon number 328 in Volume 6 of his New Park Street ministry struck me particularly. Based on Mark 11:24, he entitled the message *True Prayer ... True Power*. His first point was obvious, yet one I had overlooked:

> To make prayer of any value there should be definite objects for which to plead. We often ramble in our prayers after this, that and the other and we get nothing because we do not really desire anything ... We are like one who goes to a shop and does not know what articles he should procure ... Imagine an archer shooting with his bow and not knowing where the mark is!

Having dealt with a matter that seems relatively obvious, Spurgeon suddenly lurches into a most complex subject, one that confuses many Christians who are truly seeking God in prayer—

the relationship between our prayers and God's sovereign will. If God has purposed a certain thing to take place what is the point of me praying about it? If he will do it anyway, why exert myself to seek it? Or what if he has decided against the thing that I am so urgently requesting? I make no apologies for an extended quotation from this passage as I regard it as one of the most significant pieces on prayer to be found anywhere in Christian literature, and one that has had a profound effect on my own life:

> Prayer is the grandest power in the entire universe; it has a more omnipotent force than electricity, attraction, gravitation or any other of those secret forces which men have called by names, but which they do not understand. Prayer has as palpable, as true, as sure, as invariable an influence over the entire universe as any of the laws of nature. When a man really prays it is not a question whether God will hear him or not, he must hear him; not because there is any compulsion in the prayer, but there is a sweet and blessed compulsion in the promise. God has promised to hear prayer and he will perform his promise. As he is the most high and true God, he cannot deny himself. Oh! to think of this; that you, a puny creature, may stand here and speak to God, and through God may move all the worlds …
>
> The ear of God himself will listen and the hand of God himself will yield to your will. There is nothing, I repeat, there is no force so tremendous, no energy so marvellous, as the energy with which God has endowed every man, who like Jacob can wrestle, like Israel can prevail with him in prayer. Unless the Eternal will swerve from his word, unless the oath which he has given shall be revoked, and he himself shall cease to be what he is, 'We know we have the petitions that we desired of him.'[17]

Unanswered prayer

By 1867 the immediate power of the 1859 revival was on the

wane. What then of the many unanswered prayers, Spurgeon's congregations were asking? Some had prayed hard and long for the salvation of those whom they loved: a husband, a son or daughter, a friend and yet nothing had happened. In fact it often seemed that the one prayed for appeared harder than ever, more indifferent, more careless. Had Spurgeon any words of explanation or encouragement to address to such concerns?

In February of that year Spurgeon had preached a sermon which he entitled *Unstaggering Faith,* based on Romans 4:19–21 where Abraham 'staggered not' at God's promise that a son should be born to him and Sarah, a son from whose family blessing would come to the whole world. The thing was impossible in normal physical terms for Abraham was one hundred years old and Sarah was ninety. From these verses Spurgeon drew important principles:

> With regard to the object upon which our faith is exercised it is most probable that we shall be made to feel our own weakness and even our personal death; we shall be brought very low, even into an utter self-despair of the matter as considered in ourselves. We shall be made to see that the mercy we are seeking from God is a thing impossible with man. It is very probable that difficulties will rise before us till they are enough to overwhelm us, not only one range of mountainous impossibilities, but another will be seen towering up behind the first, till we are pressed beyond measure and led to an utter despair of the matter as considered in ourselves.

> At such a crisis, if God the Holy Spirit is working with mighty power within us, we shall still believe that the divine promise will be fulfilled … It remains with God to find ways and means, not ourselves; we shall cast the burden of fulfilling the promise upon him with whom it naturally rests and go on in steady, holy, confident joy looking for the end of our faith and patiently pleading until we reach it.

Such words brought great encouragement to me personally as I had been praying for some unbelieving friends, and yet they remained as indifferent as ever. It was with real tenacity that I laid hold of these words and memorized the lines so that more than thirty years later I can still turn to them easily among the many thousands of pages of Spurgeon's sermons. Understandably Paul preferred no markings on his books, so it was vital to me to remember where I could find them again. Further words from this same sermon have been a great comfort:

> Remember that to trust God in the light is nothing, but to trust him in the dark, that is faith. To believe that all shall go well when outward providences blow softly is any fool's play, but to believe that it must and shall be well when storms and tempests are round about you, and you are blown farther and farther from the harbour of your desire—this is a work of grace.[18]

With what exquisite pleasure?

I did not see the conversion of that couple for whom I had prayed and have now lost touch with them, but prayers can have a long-dated fulfilment with God, and perhaps not until we reach the eternal city will we know whether certain friends or relatives for whom we prayed were eventually converted. I am reminded of the words of John Grimshaw, only son of William Grimshaw of Haworth, who died just three years after his father. Unbelieving, immoral and feckless, young John had paid little regard to his father's sermons and admonitions but was soundly converted shortly after his father's death. As he died he exclaimed, 'What will my father say when he sees I am in heaven?' And Grimshaw himself once wrote 'With what exquisite pleasure … will parents departed hence rejoice over the conversion of their children whom they left behind in their sins?'

Despite the apparent disappointment with my friends, there

were many extraordinary evidences of God's hand at work amongst the young people of our church—many later becoming men and women of faith—demonstrating the reality of that work of grace. Our own three older sons were each converted at different times during that period. In the local community there were also some remarkable conversions. One sermon preached on Mark 1:15 'The kingdom of God is at hand' was especially memorable. Certainly it seemed as if that kingdom was so near we could almost reach up and touch it. Why then did the vision fade, for fade it did? I do not know. But the effect left on many who remember those days has remained. Some lines I wrote at the time express this thought:

Once I felt God's day arising,
felt him drawing near;
glory trembling on the threshold,
singing in the air.

Yes, I sipped the wine of heaven:
I can taste it yet;
sweet intoxicating gladness—
how can I forget?

When darkness veils his lovely face

*T*hroughout this time Paul was unwell. The serious stress he was suffering lasted for more than four years. During 1978 and early 1979 he struggled on with his preaching ministry, but eventually had to give up and would not be able to resume on a regular basis until the autumn of 1983.

As already mentioned, this period of trial also encompassed some of the most profound blessings of my life, blessings which ran alongside the deep anxieties and sorrow. Once again, as I look through the notebooks in which I recorded thoughts from those days, I find that hymns and verses from various poems formed a significant comfort. One of the books my mother had passed on to me had the simple title, *Hymns of Ter Steegen*,[19] *Suso and Others* and was translated from the German by Frances Bevan. I have never discovered who the 'Others' were except by their initials, such as T. P. and T. G., but their poems are beautiful and spoke to me in a special way. Words my mother had underlined had clearly been precious to her, and with the sad loss of her own two little boys, I can well understand why. In lines on *Our great High Priest*, T. P. had written:

Still his piercèd hands will finish
All the work of love begun.

And he concludes that hymn with these words:

He who led them through the desert,
Watched and guided day by day,
Turned the flinty rocks to water,
Made them brooks beside the way—
He will bring them where the fountains
Fresh and flowing from above;
Still throughout the endless ages,
Serving in the joy of love.

Such lines turned my thoughts away from my own troubles to the griefs and pain that the Saviour suffered for his people, putting my own into perspective.

The Bride

These poets lived in days of social unrest and constant wars—the War of the Austrian Succession which broke out in 1740 embroiled much of continent of Europe in eight years of strife. This was followed by the great Seven Years War from 1756 onwards. Little wonder then that their thoughts and hopes were fixed on that 'better country' where strife and sorrow are gone for ever. This echoed my own thoughts at this time as I read and reread their verses. Perhaps my favourite was one by P. G. called *The Bride*. In it he imagines the Bridegroom, Christ, watching and waiting from heaven for his bride, the church, to come home to him. He watches as she travels slowly through the desert of this life, drawing ever nearer home—and can never be satisfied until she is with him at last:

There amidst the love and glory he is waiting yet;
On his hands a name is graven he can ne'er forget.

There amidst the songs of heaven, sweeter to his ear
Is the footfall through the desert, ever drawing near.

There, made ready, are the mansions, radiant, still and fair,
But the Bride, the Father gave him, yet is wanting there.

Then the Bridegroom can wait no longer, so he runs to meet his Bride:

Who is this who comes to meet me on the desert way
As the morning star foretelling God's unclouded day?

He is it who came to win me on the cross of shame;
In his glory, well I know him, evermore the same.

O the blessed joy of meeting, all the desert past!
O the wondrous words of greeting he shall speak at last!

He and I together entering those fair courts above,
He and I together sharing all the Father's love.

Such words were a real consolation in those days. At times I nearly sank beneath the burden that had been placed on me. Not only had I a seriously ill husband, but four exuberant boys to keep quiet when their Dad needed complete rest. How I missed my daughter, now away at college! Such comments as these litter my personal accounts: 'Much cast down in spirit, greatly fearing the way will be too hard for me …' But the way was not too hard. How often God gives what he requires of us, and the support and love of the church fellowship, together with the ministry of the various visiting preachers provided unexpected strength for each days' demands.

Perhaps most precious of all at this time was a personal visit from Dr Martyn Lloyd-Jones, now over eighty years of age. Between preaching engagements at our church he spent time with me and put his finger unerringly on the source of Paul's distress—a highly strung temperament and more importantly a vicious attack of Satan to destroy a ministry that was experiencing unusual blessings from God. As that noble servant of the Lord Jesus Christ left me, we both knew we would not meet again in this world. He shook my hand warmly and said just five words—words to which I clung in the days ahead: 'Remember the love of God.'

The Olney Hymns

While the hymns of Tersteegen and his friends lifted my eyes to the heavenly city and the final triumph of God's kingdom and his people, a very different collection of hymns proved far more significant in days when the situation seemed to overwhelm me. These were the poems written by John Newton and William Cowper, known as *The Olney Hymns*. Far different in their personal backgrounds, these two eighteenth-century poets and friends had planned a hymnbook together for the use of Newton's Olney congregation. But owing to Cowper's long depressive illness his contribution to the book, both of hymns and poems, only amounted to sixty-eight pieces, while Newton himself contributed two hundred and eighty-one items.

Lines by Newton based on the promise God made to the Apostle Paul have been a support to countless men and women it times of need: 'My grace is sufficient for you, for my strength is made perfect in weakness'[20] Newton wrote tellingly,

Oppressed with unbelief and sin,
Fightings without and fears within,
While earth and hell with force combined,
Assault and terrify my mind.

What strength have I against such foes,
Such hosts and legions to oppose?
Alas! I tremble, faint and fall:
Lord, save me, or I give up all.

Thus sorely pressed, I sought the Lord,
To give me some sweet cheering word;
Again I sought and yet again;
I waited long, but not in vain.

It was a cheering word indeed!
Exactly suited to my need;
'Sufficient for thee is my grace;
Thy weakness my great power displays.'

Now I despond and mourn no more,
I welcome all I feared before:
Though weak, I'm strong; though troubled blest,
For Christ's own power shall on me rest.

A number of Newton's poems deal with what has been called The Argument of Faith, that is, a reasoning from the greater to the less, from a promise we know to be true to the smaller matter which is troubling us at the moment. For example, God 'who did not spare His own Son, but delivered Him up for us all, how shall He not with Him also freely give us all things?'[21] It then follows logically that:

If to Jesus for relief,
My soul has fled by prayer
Why should I give way to grief

Or heart consuming care?
Are not all things in his hand,
Has he not his promise passed?
Will he then regardless stand
And let me sink at last?

If he shed his precious blood
To bring me to the fold,
Can I think that lesser good
He ever will withhold?
Satan, vain is your device,
Here my hope rests well assured;
In that grand redemption price
I see the whole secured.

Precious Brooks

And the books! Once again during these years I began rummaging
around in Paul's special bookcase where he kept works by Puritan and other older writers. I drew out several volumes of *The Works of Thomas Brooks.* Born in 1608, Brooks' ministry fell in the troubled period of the English Civil Wars, and like Richard Baxter he was ejected from his living in 1662. I knew little about church history at that stage, but I was intrigued by the quaint titles of Brooks' printed sermons. *An Ark for*

THE COMPLETE WORKS

OF

T H O M A S   B R O O K S.

Edited, with Memoir,

BY THE REV. ALEXANDER BALLOCH GROSART,

LIVERPOOL.

VOL. III.

CONTAINING:

THE UNSEARCHABLE RICHES OF CHRIST.
A CABINET OF JEWELS.

all God's Noahs—in a gloomy, stormy day: that matched my mood; it was an exposition of Lamentations 3:24, 'The Lord is my portion … therefore will I hope in him.' But it was two other sermons that spoke directly into my present need. One was called *The Mute Christian under the Smarting Rod*—strange title. I discovered Brooks was preaching on words in Psalm 39:9, 'I opened not my mouth, because thou didst it'. C. H. Spurgeon says of this Puritan preacher, 'Brooks scatters stars with both hands' and in this sermon that was certainly the case. Urging Christians to accept the troubles God allows into our lives with a quiet spirit rather than with a storm of grief and distress, Brooks writes, 'Grace differs nothing from glory but in name: grace is glory in the bud, and glory is grace in the flower … therefore the more grace here, the more glory hereafter—the higher in grace, the higher in glory.' This was a new thought to me. Brooks seemed to be saying, 'If we can lay hold on the grace of God to accept our sorrows and difficulties here in this life, the joy awaiting us in the life to come will be richer and fuller.'

But a sermon I discovered in volume 5 of Brooks' works was the most significant help of any I had read up until that point. Its long title alone gives the essence of its teaching: *The Signal Presence of God with his people in their greatest troubles, deepest distresses and most deadly dangers.* Surely this more than covered any situation I might be facing. So I copied out several of the most memorable passages:

> Troubles will be no troubles; distresses will be no distresses, dangers will be no dangers, if you can but secure the presence of God with you. Mountains will be molehills, stabs at the heart will be but scratches upon the hand, if the divine presence be with you. God's signal presence will turn storms into calms, winter nights into summer days, prisons into palaces, banishments into enlargements … No afflictions, no trials can make it night with the Christian, so long as he enjoys the presence of God with his spirit.

In a sentence, Brooks was able to say:

> God's gracious presence makes every condition a little heaven to the believing soul.[22]

I rest on his unchanging grace

*I*little realized when I copied out those last words from Thomas Brooks about every condition being a little heaven to the believer how much I would be called upon to prove whether they were really true in my own experience or just a beautifully phrased thought. In July 1981 Paul resigned from the pastorate of the Shepshed Evangelical Church having little prospect of a sufficient recovery of health to resume his ministry in the foreseeable months.

The church had been built up since that sad break with the Baptist church in 1969. Having lost all our buildings, we had worshipped first in a hall then known as the Adult School Hall—a building that had seen better days. Then in 1970 we were able to secure building land in the middle of the town, an ideal situation for a new church and surely a provision from God. While finance was being gathered, plans drawn up and an attractive building erected, the small congregation moved to a seldom used Strict Baptist Chapel known as Bethesda Chapel, hidden away among trees near the schools our children attended. The roof leaked, the decorations were poor, but we soldiered on and at last in June 1975 were able to open our new building with Dr Martyn Lloyd-Jones preaching on the first Sunday. We were deeply conscious of God's hand of blessing on the work and looked forward in eager anticipation to future days of the grace of God on our town and community. Nor were we disappointed: as outlined earlier, these were significant years of unusual blessing.

For me personally that resignation from the ministry in 1981 had all the hallmarks of a bereavement. A church fellowship does indeed become 'family' to the Christian. In a recent publication by Steve Timmis entitled *I wish Jesus hadn't said that … but I'm really glad he did*[23] Timmis comments on the relationship between our biological families and our church family. In reference to Christ's words, 'Whoever does the will of God, he is my brother and sister and mother,'[24] he maintains cogently that the union we enjoy with fellow believers in Christ is something that supersedes even family ties: 'The supernatural work of grace which binds the family of God together in Christ is something altogether stunning,' he concludes.

Paul's resignation from the pastorate, of course, meant that as soon as he was well enough we would need to leave Shepshed and seek a new opening for his ministry. We had been seventeen years in the town and for me it was the only real home I had ever known. In the event two further years would elapse before we were able to leave, and these were years when I was thrown back on God's 'unchanging grace' in a new way. Once again it was to books that I turned as an unfailing source of strength and consolation.

It would be wrong to suggest that my response to my situation was all spiritual and correct. Far from it. A strong current of idolatry fuelled the intensity of my reactions. The human heart is constantly prone to the sin of idolatry: maybe not idols of wood and clay but the idols of comfort, affections and joys that bind us to the things of this earth.[25] I was being asked to prove the reality of that experience given to me in November 1978 when I learnt that earthly joys are a bonus of grace, but true and lasting joy 'comes in the morning.'

Loosening our hold

Many books clamour for a mention as sources of both correction and comfort during these days, but perhaps six lines from the pen of Gerhard Tersteegen—to give him his full name—form a succinct summary:

> Gently loosens he your hold
> On the treasured former things—
> Loves and joys that were of old,
> Shapes to which the spirit clings—
> And alone, alone he stands,
> Stretching forth beseeching hands.

I was having to learn that Christ will have no rivals in our affections and more than this, that he is abundantly sufficient in himself to satisfy the deepest longings of the heart. A small book I came across that summer in 1981 blended with Tersteegen's lines and proved a great support. Called *Midnight Harmonies,* it was by Octavius Winslow—eighth child of Mary Winslow. Written in 1850, it appears to have been occasioned by his sister's serious illness and is dedicated to her. Somewhat flowery in true Victorian style and even a little wordy, *Midnight Harmonies* fitted perfectly my state of mind at that time. Our copy was faded, its back broken and its pages falling loose—a book that could withstand all weathers as it accompanied me to many hidden corners of the farm on which we were staying during our summer holiday!

Basing his comments on verses such as Job 35:10 where Elihu tells Job that God gives 'songs in the night,' Winslow seeks to draw comfort out of those times of darkness in the life of a believer which God uses to teach lessons that we are slow to learn in normal circumstances:

> O Lord, that is a blessed night of weeping in which I can sing of your sustaining grace, your enlivening presence, of your unfaltering faithfulness, of your tender love ... With not one ingredient in my cup of sorrows could I have safely dispensed. All was needed. O Lord, I dare not ask that it pass my lips untasted for I may find a token of your love beneath the bitter draught ... I asked you to possess my entire heart, and you have touched my idol. I asked that I might drink more deeply of the fountain of your love and you have broken my cistern. But it is well; it is all well. Though you slay me, I will trust in you.[26]

Again, hymns spoke to me with a message that was hard to miss. One by Samuel Rodigast, translated from the German by Catherine Winkworth was a case in point:

All that my God ordains is right:
He never will deceive me;
He leads me by a proper path,
I know he will not leave me.
    I take, content,
      What God has sent;
His hand can turn my griefs away,
And patiently I wait his day.[27]

But the greatest influence

But the book that was the greatest influence of all on me, not just at this time but arguably upon my whole subsequent life was *The Letters of Samuel Rutherford*. I had been familiar from childhood days with Anne Ross Cousin's great hymn, based on some of Rutherford's last words:

The sands of time are sinking,
The dawn of heaven breaks;
The summer morn I've sighed for,
The fair sweet morn awakes.
Dark, dark hath been the midnight,
But dayspring is at hand,
And glory, glory dwelleth
In Immanuel's land.

The hymn actually runs to nineteen verses, each one weaving together words and phrases found in Rutherford's *Letters*. I already knew much of it by heart and challenged our young son, Simon, then about eleven years of age, to learn it and recite all nineteen verses to me for the princely reward of £5.00—a handsome sum in those days! He rose to the challenge admirably and apart from the odd stumble here and there had mastered the hymn. Sadly for him his stumbles were penalized and he has recently reminded me that he only received £4.75!

Beyond all praise of men

I had also owned and valued a small collection of excerpts from the *Letters*, selected by Ellen Lister and published under the title *The Loveliness of Christ*.[28] But I had never before seen the whole collection. C. H. Spurgeon says of these letters:

> Rutherford is beyond all praise of men. Like a strong-winged eagle he soars into the highest heaven and with unblenched eye he looks into the mystery of divine love. There is to us something mysterious, awe-creating and superhuman about Rutherford's letters.

Strong recommendation indeed! A friend had lent me a copy

of *The Letters*, and then, seeing how much I was valuing them, my mother gave me her copy. With its blue cover somewhat faded by life in the tropics, this book became a treasure indeed. The first thing I noticed was the name of its original owner, Fred Mitchell. A most outstanding and godly Christian man, Mitchell had been the Home Director of the mission with which my parents had served in the Far East. Then known as the CIM, the mission and all its personnel had been expelled from China in 1951. My father, Stanley Rowe, burdened for the Chinese people, had applied to return to the Far East as soon as the Mission decided it was safe to send workers back to other far eastern countries such as Malaysia, Thailand and Indonesia. And it was Fred Mitchell who oversaw my parents' placement in one of the New Villages in Malaysia early in 1952. Although only a child of thirteen, I knew and respected Mitchell and like many others was deeply shocked to hear of his death just a year later in a Comet crash. The de Havilland aircraft, in service for just a year, was the first commercial jet aircraft to fly. Fred Mitchell had been visiting my parents and others in Malaysia and was returning to England on the Comet. Without warning the plane had disintegrated in mid-flight, flinging its wreckage across paddy fields not far from Calcutta. All on board were killed. Metal fatigue in the cabin was later blamed for the catastrophe.

Untold consolation

Knowing about his untimely death, I studied Mitchell's underlinings in my copy of the book, one that had been given by his widow to my mother.[29] As I read, I understood why *The Letters* were so significant to this Christian man and to hundreds of others since its first publication in 1664, three years after Rutherford's own death. At that time it brought untold consolation to harassed and fugitive Christians, men and women known as the Covenanters, who were being hounded to and fro like animals during days of relentless persecution in Scotland, following the Restoration of Charles II to the throne in 1660: days known as the Killing Times.

Samuel Rutherford was born in 1600 in the Scottish village of Nisbet and was probably about twenty-four before he was converted. Three years later he accepted the invitation of Sir John Gordon of Lochinvar, later Lord Kenmure, to become the first minister of a newly-built church in the idyllic village of Anwoth, just outside Gatehouse-of-Fleet in south west Scotland. The small fair-haired preacher's ministry soon attracted attention even in that out-of-the-way spot. Described as 'one of the most moving and affectionate preachers of his time,' Rutherford's reputation drew both responsive hearers and strong hostility. His enemies won—or thought they had. The Bishop of Galloway was anxious to stamp out all traces of the Reformation in his parishes and bring the churches back to pre-Reformation forms authorized by the High Churchman, Archbishop Laud. Brought to trial by an ecclesiastical court, Rutherford was stripped of his ministry, and exiled to Aberdeen under house arrest. But he was not silenced: during the next twenty-two months he wrote many of his matchless letters from his Aberdeen exile to his parishioners in Anwoth and elsewhere. He encouraged, cajoled, advised and comforted his friends and it is these letters that were eventually gathered together and published, forming the bulk of the book I now held in my hands.

To Robert Gordon, from the parish adjoining Anwoth, and whom Rutherford clearly knew well, Rutherford writes:

Oh, what owe I to the file, to the hammer, to the furnace of my Lord Jesus! Who hath now let me see how good the wheat is that goeth through his mill and his oven to be made bread for his table. Grace tried is better than grace, and it is more than grace; it is glory in its infancy … Why should I start at the plough of my Lord, that maketh deep furrows on my soul? I know he is no idle husbandman, he purposes a crop … How blind are my adversaries, who sent me to a banqueting house, to a house of wine, to the lovely feasts of my lovely Lord, and not to a prison or a place of exile.

If Rutherford could regard his place of exile, his expulsion from his ministry in Anwoth which he elsewhere describes as his 'second heaven' as 'a banqueting house', then surely, I ought to be able to see that leaving my home, my friends and my church could be in God's purposes to enrich and not to impoverish me. But I found it hard to lay hold of such courage and trust in the purposes of God.

As Paul's health began gradually to improve during 1982 and 1983, he started to look seriously at possible places where he could start his ministry over again. Slowly I became reconciled to the idea of moving from Shepshed, but sadly, my reluctance must have been of little encouragement to Paul at that time. At last I reached the position where I said to the Lord in prayer, 'Lord, I will go anywhere you want me to go. I will even go to Cornwall if that is your will, but please, please don't send me back to the north of England.' My memories of our experiences in Northallerton were too raw for me to even consider such a possibility at that point.

Wider purposes

Not long afterwards a letter came for Paul from Hull inviting him to preach at a small church in the city—a church that had suffered, a church that needed a ministry of comfort and consolation. My heart sank. Could this really be true? Could God be crossing all my earthly desires? Again, lines from Tersteegen's verses expressed my thoughts as I struggled to accept the situation:

Across the will of nature
Leads on the path of God;
Not where the flesh delighteth
The steps of Jesus trod.

If now the path be narrow
And steep and rough and lone,
If crags and tangles cross it,
Praise God, we will go on!

Or as Samuel Rutherford expressed it, 'When the Lord's blessed will bloweth across your desires, it is best in humility to strike sail to him and be willing to be led any way our Lord pleaseth ... Ye know not what the Lord is working out of this, but ye shall know it hereafter.'[30]

The call from Hull was accepted and to Hull we would go. It was 1983 almost four years since Paul had been in regular ministry. How would we cope, how leave the town that had been home for nineteen years? As that bold green and white 'For Sale' board was erected in our garden, perhaps the hardest aspect of all was the 'loss' of three members of our family. Esther was to start work in London, Jerry, who was nineteen, had a steady job in Loughborough, but hardest of all was the plight of sixteen-year-old Oliver. These were the days when apprenticeships were rare as gold dust and Ollie, as he was now known, had gained a coveted joinery apprenticeship with a Shepshed firm that would give him an excellent training. How could we leave our home-loving boy and place him in digs at such a young age? It is a question I still find hard to answer. Surely, the God in whom he trusted would care and provide—to this we clung. Only the two younger boys would accompany us to Hull—the family shrunk from seven to four.

Words which Rutherford wrote to Lady Kenmure soon after the death of her third infant daughter often rang in my ears during those days:

Build your nest upon no tree here; for ye see God hath sold the forest to death and every tree whereupon we would rest is ready to be cut down, to the end we may fly and mount up and build upon the Rock.[31]

These words challenged all my preconceptions. Certainly, I had been 'building my nest' in that small rural town. Maybe God had wider purposes for my life and wanted to 'cut down' that support on which I had been relying that I might build more securely on the Rock.

And then I began to write …

*A*lexander Whyte, highly acclaimed minister of the Free Church of Scotland in the nineteenth and early twentieth centuries, maintained that all dying Christians should have a copy of *The Letters of Samuel Rutherford* tucked under their pillows. The thought made me smile for such a bulky volume would hardly be an easy or comfortable companion under one's pillow at such a time. But the reasoning behind the suggestion was obvious. Rutherford was so absorbed with the glories of the world to come and the joys awaiting the Christian, that his words can lift our eyes beyond the sorrow, the pain and the parting, easing the circumstances we face at such a fragile time.

Whyte must have had in mind words such as these which Rutherford wrote to Lady Kenmure at a time of sickness (even though she was only thirty-one):

Be content to wade through the waters betwixt you and glory with him, holding his hand fast, for he knoweth all the fords. Howbeit you may be ducked, but ye cannot drown, being in his company … Be not afraid, therefore, when ye come even to the black and swelling river of death, to put in your foot and wade after him … If ye knew what he is preparing for you ye would be too glad … ye shall then say, 'Four and twenty hours' abode in this place is worth three score and ten years of sorrow upon earth'.[32]

An enormous contrast

However, I had a far different situation to face as we moved to our new home in Hull. The house was sizeable with three large receptions rooms and five bedrooms and seemed to swallow up our reduced family. A Victorian terraced house, it stood on a long straight avenue, lined with tall lime trees. In former days 'The Avenues', as the four parallel avenues were known locally, had once been the homes of merchants and business men, and then of intellectuals and academics of different shades. Some, like ours, were initially designed to include 'servants' quarters'. Now the area had fallen into a measure of decline and many of the larger houses were used as bed-sits, student accommodation and boarding houses. Each spacious room in our new home had high ceilings and tall skirting boards in true Victorian style. At last Paul had room for all his books, and we could even claim several 'book-free' rooms.

We were warmly and kindly welcomed at the church and everything was done to make the transition straightforward. But the early months were far from easy. I knew our son Ollie was deeply unhappy and missing his home, but there was nothing I could do about it. The enormous contrast between a small rural town and city life was hard to handle. There I had grown to know so many but here everyone went about his or her own business, and the world seemed strangers to us and we to the world. Little did I imagine at that time that God in his wisdom was doing more, far more, for me in those very circumstances than I could possibly know. He was breaking open the tight web of insularity that I had been carefully weaving around myself for nineteen years, possibly a compensation for the childhood years of homelessness that I had known.

Sharing treasures

Once again Samuel Rutherford had words exactly suited to my need as he wrote to Lady Kenmure. Her three infant daughters had died in quick succession, and then her husband had also died. At the time of his death she was expecting their fourth child, and when young John was born she clung to him tenaciously. Rutherford feared for her. What if this child were taken as well? And then his fears were realized when the four-year-old boy also died. Even Rutherford was baffled by the disaster, but wrote to the bereaved mother with tenderness and yet with resolve:

> Madam, subscribe to the Almighty's will; put your hand to the pen and let the cross of your Lord Jesus have your submissive and resolute AMEN … And I shall believe for my part that he mindeth to distil heaven out of this loss … for wisdom devised it, and love laid it on, and Christ owneth it as his own and putteth your shoulder beneath only a piece of it …

Brave words indeed and I could not begin to compare my circumstances with the sorrows which that mother was bearing.

With typical enthusiasm I began to share these treasures I was discovering in *The Letters* with my new friends. But I was baffled. I received only puzzled looks and polite smiles in reply. What was wrong? Then I realised there were two main obstacles that stood in the way of an appreciation of the writings of this quaint and graphic Scottish Covenanter. First was the archaic language: the 'ye's and 'eth's sprinkled liberally throughout formed an obvious barrier. Then Rutherford's poetic imagery as he leapt from one metaphor to another without explanation made his words hard to follow. How then could I share these spiritual gems with my friends? Then I hit on an idea. I would put Rutherford's words and concepts into the form of metre and rhyme, simplifying it yet retaining the truths. The above words to Lady Kenmure I rendered as follows:

> O child of God, this grief
> That bows your spirit low
> Is yours but half, for Christ himself
> Still shares his people's woe.
>
> His wisdom planned it out,
> Then bore it on his heart
> Till gently on your untried back
> Love laid the lesser part.
>
> So take it all with joy,
> Together bear the cross,
> For while you suffer he distils
> A heaven from your loss.
>
> Beneath his secret will
> Subscribe with ready pen,
> Add to this sorrow God has sent
> A resolute 'AMEN'.

Encouragement to continue

Having hit on this idea I continued to transpose some of my favourite passages in *The Letters* into verse form and found joy in doing so. With some uncertainty I showed my work to Paul who thought it was worth sending to the Rev. Iain Murray of the Banner of Truth Trust to see if he thought it held any potential for publication. Receiving a positive response was a great encouragement to continue the work. Mr Murray also suggested I should try to write biographical sketches of Rutherford's first correspondents, showing the relevance of the letters to their individual circumstances. As I had done no serious writing work since my school essays, this appeared a daunting task. But as I worked I had a dawning understanding that the difficulties, separations and griefs both of the past and of recent years had been designed by God as a preparation for this very thing. As Chuck Coulson said of his conversion when incarcerated in an Alabama prison in 1974 for his involvement in the Watergate scandal, 'My great defeat is what God is using,' so, like him, I too could say, 'If out of my sins and sorrows God has any purposes of blessing for others, he will enable me to do it.'

Grace in Winter

At last the work was complete: it contained thirty-six extracts from Rutherford's *Letters* rendered into verse form, with sixteen biographical sketches of the correspondents to whom the letters were addressed, with one on Rutherford himself. A friend contributed five beautiful photographs he had taken of the area around Anwoth where Rutherford had ministered, while three other photographs, taken by friends, were included to illustrate the verses themselves. The foreword was written by the late Jock Purves, himself the author of a moving book on the martyrdom of some of the noblest of the Covenanters. That foreword was one of the last things he wrote, and not long before he died he sent me a letter in which he quoted some of Rutherford's words, 'My faith hath no bed to lie on save Omnipotency,' and after them he wrote in block capitals, 'MARVELLOUS, WONDERFUL! I think about it all the time.' Here was a Christian who had certainly heeded Alexander Whyte's injunction.

The title of the book, was to be *Grace in Winter*, a shortened form of Rutherford's own words to Lady Culross, 'I see grace groweth best in winter.' It was published in 1989 by The Banner of Truth as a slim hardback. Holding the beautifully produced book in my hands, I could at last say with the Psalmist, as I looked back on the path along which the Lord had led me, 'As for God, his way is perfect.'

To be a pilgrim

*P*erhaps the most important lesson that I had learnt in our move from Shepshed to Hull was that I must never again hold any earthly home or even my friends so dear that I would be reluctant to move away if that should be God's will. True, our Midlands home was where all our family had grown up, where friendships were close and strong and where memories of shared joys and sorrows were deeply etched on our minds. But now I resolved to live as a 'pilgrim', or in more mundane terms, to regard each earthly home in which I might live as if it were only a 'bed and breakfast' place, a stop-over on the journey to my real and eternal home. Once again Rutherford, who had himself been wrenched from his Anwoth home into exile in Aberdeen, expressed it with vivid imagery:

> We smell of the smoke of this lower house of the earth because our hearts and thoughts are here … God be thanked that we have

many things that so stroke us against the hair that we may pray, 'God keep our better home, God bless our Father's house …' I am sure that this is the best fruit of the cross … when we cry the more that God would send a fair wind to land us, hungered and oppressed strangers, at the door of our Father's house, which is now made in Christ our kindly heritage.[33]

The fourteen years we were to spend in Hull were good years. Paul's health steadily improved, and he had the joy of seeing permanent fruit for his ministry, with some significant conversions and numbers attending Kingston Evangelical Church steadily building up. Students from the university came to us, some for short periods, others for the full course of their degree studies. Overseas students enriched our congregation and some have remained permanent friends.

John Bunyan

I missed the three older members of the family sorely and much time was spent on the phone as I tried to keep in contact with each one. Times when they visited, first on their own and then later with their families were joyful occasions. With just the two younger boys at home, I now had much more time to read. I turned to the six battered volumes of the *Complete Works of John Bunyan* Paul had earlier given me and now began to read portions of these books in earnest, little knowing how much they would influence my future thinking and spiritual development.

I was familiar with the story of *The Pilgrim's Progress* from my preschool days when I had watched my father use his flannelgraph lessons to teach children the story during his missionary work in far off Ningxia, north-west China. Now, as I flicked through the pages of my volumes, I discovered that Bunyan had written at least fifty-five other titles, though I have never met anyone who can truthfully say he has read through all of them. Some deal with controversies which raged in the seventeenth century, but among them, hidden in the large double columned pages, lie priceless treasures of Christian wisdom that have greatly enriched my own life.

To write a biography of Bunyan is a daunting task, as I indeed found it to be. Apart from the story of his conversion and early imprisonment in *Grace Abounding to the Chief of Sinners*, he tells us little about his own experiences. Never does he divulge the names of his family members, nor any details of his circumstances in later life—all must be gleaned from secondary sources. But in many of his lesser-known works we may discover personal glimpses. So in a sermon entitled *The Jerusalem Sinner Saved, or Good news for the Vilest of Men*, preached in the last year of his life, he says:

> I speak by experience. I was one of those lousy ones, one of the great sin breeders. I infected all the youth of the town where I was born, with all manner of youthful vanities. The neighbours counted me so; my practice proved me so: wherefore Christ Jesus took me first, and taking me first, the contagion was much allayed all the town over. When God made me sigh, they would hearken and say, 'What's the matter with John?' When I went out to seek the bread of life, some of them would follow, and the rest be put into a muse.

This reminds us of *The Pilgrim's Progress*. When Christian fled the City of Destruction, some, like Obstinate and Pliable, followed while the rest of the town was 'put in a muse'.

Bunyan's preaching style was warm, passionate, full of pathos and tender pleading. His approach to those who listened was direct and challenging. One who heard him could say that his words made them feel, 'as if an angel had touched their souls with a coal of holy fire from the altar'. Little wonder then that vast crowds would gather at five in the morning before their working day began to hear this preacher.

Historical backdrop

Bunyan's story can only be understood against the backdrop of his life circumstances and the appalling persecution that he and others experienced during the period that followed the Restoration to the English throne of Charles II. The newly installed government, called the Cavalier Parliament, was bent on revenge against Puritans and non-conformists for all that the Royalists had suffered during the Civil War. It was determined to stamp out any worship outside the Established Church, a resolve which led directly to the 1662 *Act of Uniformity* with its rigid demand that all preachers declare their complete agreement with every statement in the newly revised *Book of Common Prayer*. The deadline for conformity was 24 August 1662, later called Black Bartholomew's Day, a day when 2000 ministers and teachers were evicted from their livings for conscience sake.

But at least two years before that date the Bedford authorities where Bunyan now lived had been determined to stop him preaching. His powerful and effective ministry was drawing crowds wherever he went. As he wrote:

> My great desire in the fulfilling of my ministry was to get into the darkest places of the country, even amongst those people that were farthest off profession … because my spirit leaned most after awakening and converting work.[34]

This had raised the antagonism of clerics and magistrates alike until Bunyan could report, 'The doctors and priests of the country did open their mouths wide against me.' Not only did they vilify him but they searched for means to silence him. Because no law as yet existed against lay preaching or religious gatherings outside the parish churches, his opponents resurrected an obsolete Elizabethan law against such meetings in an attempt to catch him.

Incarceration

At a farmhouse in Lower Samsell not far from Bedford, a nervous group of men and women had gathered to hear Bunyan preach even though they had heard a rumour that a warrant had been issued for his arrest. Courageously Bunyan still determined to preach though he knew the stakes were high. What would his young wife Elizabeth do if he were arrested? Married to John after the death of Mary, his first wife, she was pregnant with her first child. How would she cope with caring on her own for her four stepchildren and a new infant as well? But Bunyan cast himself on God for strength and stood firm.

When magistrates burst into the meeting that very night he was arrested, faced a kangaroo court on 6 January 1661 and at the age of thirty-two was incarcerated in Bedford County Jail where he remained for the next twelve years, until he was forty-four—unable to preach or support his family. Elizabeth, probably little more than eighteen, suffered the miscarriage of their expected child on the news of his arrest and was left to care for John's family without any support apart from charity. Mary, the eldest was ten years old and blind from birth, while John's youngest child, Thomas, was still only two.

Prison conditions were atrocious: filthy and stinking, with little to lie on at night but a mat and some straw. The cold was intense and rats scuttled freely around among the dirt. A description of the state of the prisons at the time makes even the boldest heart quail: 'fit only for beasts,' was the description, and we might well add, not even fit for beasts.

Compassed with infirmities

But worse than any outward circumstances was the burden of heart Bunyan experienced as he thought of his family and above all of little blind Mary, so much in need of her father's care. It came close to breaking his spirit:

> I found myself a man, and compassed with infirmities; the parting with my wife and poor children hath oft been to me in this place as the pulling the flesh from my bones, and that not only because I am somewhat too fond of those great mercies, but also because I should have often brought to my mind the many hardships, miseries and wants that my poor family was like to meet with, should I be taken from them, especially my poor blind child, who lay nearer my heart than all I had besides.

Was he doing the right thing? Despite many misgivings, he could still give a resounding 'Yes' to that question and wrote:

> I have determined, the Almighty God being my help and shield, yet to suffer if frail life might continue so long, even until the moss shall grow upon mine eyebrows, rather than … violate my faith and principles.

His enemies had determined to silence John Bunyan. They did the reverse. For in those long years in Bedford Jail this persecuted Christian wrote many of his finest books, including *The Pilgrim's Progress*, books which have been the incalculable heritage of the church of Jesus Christ ever since. Added to this, his sufferings made him the preacher he became. Before his style was intense and sometimes harsh, but when he was released at last in 1672 and took over pastoral charge of the small Bedford Dissenting Meeting, an empathy and tenderness accompanied his words.

How then did Bunyan endure such suffering? He tells us in one succinct sentence:

> I was made to see that if ever I would suffer rightly I must first pass a sentence of death upon everything that can properly be called a thing of this life, even to reckon myself, my wife, my children, my

health, my enjoyments, and all, as dead to me and myself as dead to them.

This may seem a negative concept if John had not added one vital clause. Instead, he determined to 'live upon God who is invisible.' As I read those words, they touched me deeply, for I knew it was the same lesson that God had been teaching me too through all the varied circumstances of recent years. And in Bunyan's case his prison experiences were in his estimate an immense gain:

> He [God] can make those things that in themselves are most fearful and terrible to behold, the most pleasant, delightful and desirable things. He can make a gaol more beautiful than a palace … He can so sweeten our sufferings with the honey of his word … and [make them] so easy by the spreading of his feathers over us that we shall not be able to say that in all the world a more comfortable position can be found

Bunyan's own life was one of constant persecution. Even after being released from prison in 1672 he was in continual danger. For several years he was 'on the run' hunted from place to place because he would not stop preaching. At last in 1676 he gave himself up and was thrown back in prison once more. Had it not been for the intervention of the theologian John Owen, he might well have ended his days in prison, but was finally released in 1677.

Strangers and Pilgrims

We too grieve so often as we hear of the fearful persecution meted out to our fellow believers in other parts of the world. The concept of pilgrimage and the reward awaiting Christ's suffering people at the end of the journey was Bunyan's only consolation at times:

> To see Christ Jesus then, to see him as he is in glory, is a sight that is worth going from relations, and out of the body and through

the jaws of death to see; … to see him preparing mansion houses for those his poor ones that are now by his enemies kicked to and fro like footballs in the world. Is this not a blessed sight?[38]

Pre-eminently, therefore, John Bunyan teaches us to regard our lives as Christians as a pilgrimage from this world of sin and suffering to the Celestial City. In our materialistic age it is easy to lose sight of this dimension, but the scriptures frequently take up the image. Old Jacob tells Pharaoh that the 'years of his pilgrimage were one hundred and thirty years,' and the writer to the Hebrews speaks of the patriarchs as 'strangers and pilgrims on the earth' looking for a better country—a heavenly one. The wilderness journey of the Israelites from Egypt to the Promised Land reinforces the idea. This world is not our home and we travel to 'a city which has foundations, whose builder and maker is God.'

And this was the lesson that my move to Hull reinforced. Far from depriving me of joys that I had known, it was clearly God's purpose to liberate me to serve him better.

O love that will not let me go

Bunyan has of course immortalised the theme of pilgrimage in *The Pilgrim's Progress*. In Part 2 of that book we watch as each of his pilgrims approaches the last river, the River of Death and crosses over. So when *Mr Standfast* entered the waters he could say:

> I see myself now at the end of my journey, my toilsome days are ended. I am now going to see the head that was crowned with thorns and that face that was spit upon for me. I have lived formerly by hearsay and faith; but now I go where I shall live by sight and shall be with him in whose company I delight myself … He has held me and kept me from my iniquities, yea, my steps hath he strengthened in his way.[39]

But before his pilgrims cross over, Bunyan brings them into a land which he calls the Country of Beulah. Lying within sight of the heavenly city, Beulah is a place where:

The air was very sweet and pleasant … Yea here [the pilgrims] heard continually the singing of birds and saw every day the flowers appear in the earth … in this country the sun shineth night and day, wherefore this was beyond the Valley of the Shadow of Death and also out of reach of Giant Despair … In this land the Shining Ones commonly walked because it was on the borders of heaven.

The concept of Beulah land has caught the imagination of many Christians—a period of calm and joyful anticipation immediately before death. But is it true? In the course of my research into the lives of those about whom I have written, I have read of many who had a difficult 'crossing' as Bunyan's Christian himself did in *The Pilgrim's Progress*. Death is indeed the last enemy, but very often we may read about or witness a period of sweet peace just before the end. Once many used to gather around the bed of a dying Christian to catch some of the last things that they said. Spurgeon writes of the 'valley of the shadow of death' in his commentary on Psalm 23 in these words:

Death is not the house but the porch, not the goal but the passage to it. Dying is called a 'valley'. The storm breaks on the mountain but the valley is a place of quietude … the mountain is bleak and bare, but the valley is rich with golden sheaves, and many a saint has reaped more knowledge when he came to die than he ever knew when he lived. Death stands by the side of the highway, but only its shadow crosses our path; let us then rejoice that there is a light beyond. The shadow of a dog cannot bite; the shadow of a sword cannot kill; the shadow of death cannot destroy us.[40]

Certainly, Edward Payson, American pastor and preacher born in 1783 and living through a period of many revivals, could record in a letter to his sister when he was dying at the age of forty-four:

Were I to adopt the figurative language of Bunyan, I might date this letter, 'from the Land of Beulah' of which I have been for some weeks a happy inhabitant. The celestial city is full in my view. Its glories beam upon me, its breezes fan me … and its spirit is breathed into my heart. Nothing separates me from it but the river of death, which now appears but an insignificant rill that may be crossed at a single step, whenever God shall give permission.

Grace and Glory

Thoughts of heaven have coloured my thinking ever since that night in November 1978 recorded earlier. Yes, 'Weeping may endure for a night, but joy comes in the morning.' So when I read a book by Geerhardus Vos called *Grace and Glory*,[41] I found much that chimed with some of my own deepest convictions. Vos was born in 1881 and served as a lecturer at Princeton Seminary in New Jersey until his retirement, dying there in 1949

I have always admired anyone who says they enjoy reading the works of Geerhardus Vos, as I found his depth of thought put him way out of my reach. The cover blurb to this small book explains why. In reference to his main theological writings, we read: 'His thought is broad and deep, intellectually all-demanding but immensely rewarding for the student of Scripture.' So I little thought when I saw this book that I would find anything he wrote accessible. But I was wrong. These were not lectures as such but sermons and many were both profound and warmly devotional. One chapter in *Grace and Glory* stands out in particular. Basing his thoughts on Hebrews 11:9–10 in which we read that Abraham was 'a sojourner in the land of promise', Vos calls his chapter *Heavenly-Mindedness*.

Although 'the land of promise' for Abraham and the other patriarchs, was the literal Canaan to which he had journeyed from Ur of the Chaldees, Vos points out that these heroes of faith did not regard even Canaan as the final destination to which they were travelling but only a type of the 'better country' promised to all

God's people. In memorable words Vos says: 'Acquaintance with a fairer Canaan had stolen from their heart the love of the land that lay spread around like a garden of paradise.'

He continues,

> He who knows that for him a palace is in building does not dally with desires for improvement on a lower scale …The refusal to build an abiding habitation in a certain place must be due to the recognition that one's true permanent abode is elsewhere. The not-feeling-at-home in one country has for its inevitable counterpart home-sickness for another.'

The danger accompanying such thoughts for me is a degree of escapism from the realities and difficulties of life in this present world. The main corrective for such thinking, however, is the enormous importance of using the fleeting moments of life allowed by God to serve him while we are here. And in my own case, God has given me family to care about and allowed me the privilege of my writing work, telling of the lives and contribution of Christian men and women from previous generations. And with these privileges goes an accountability to use the time I have responsibly. These two things do not stand in contradiction to each other, rather, as Vos points out, our desires for heaven and communion with God in prayer should actually enrich our present activities and service.

> The Christian is never wholly separated from the land of promise. His tents are pitched in close view of the city of God. Heaven is present to the believer's experience in no less real a sense than Canaan with its fair hills and valleys lay close to the vision of Abraham … He was given to taste the powers of the world to come as he breathed the air of Canaan, and was refreshed by the dews descending on its fields. The roots of the Christian's life are fed from those rich perennial springs that lie deep in the recesses of converse

with God, where prayers ascend and divine graces descend, so that after each season of tryst he issues, a new man, from the secrecy of his tent. [42]

Other sermons in this gem of a book are equally enriching and challenging.

Our years in Hull came to an end in 1997 as Paul retired from the full-time ministry. We moved back to the Midlands to be in a central position for the family who were now scattered in different parts of the country. But this was not the end of Paul's ministry. He had prayed that God would give him an extra three years of opportunities to preach to compensate for those three darkest years he had 'lost' before we left Shepshed. It was a prayer God abundantly answered—in fact giving him nearly ten further years of service as he travelled up and down the country fulfilling invitations from many different churches to preach in their pulpits.

These were years when I too had opportunities to travel as I researched the lives of a number of men and women of faith. Some of our holidays were used to visit places associated with those whose stories I was covering: Selina Countess of Huntingdon, William Grimshaw of Haworth, and of course John Bunyan himself.

And still the remembrance of life as a pilgrimage simmered in the back of my mind. Then one day I received a surprising parcel from America. An elderly lady, who said she had known me as a child when I was still in China, sent me a book which she thought would interest me—a book concerning the suffering church of Jesus Christ in China.

Safely Home

I turned it over carefully in my hand—it was by an author new to me—Randy Alcorn. I learnt from the cover blurb that Alcorn had been a pastor for fourteen years and was currently living in Oregon, now the founder and director of Eternal Perspective Ministries. I was intrigued, and the more so when I discovered that this book, called *Safely Home* was actually a novel. It told of two friends, an American businessman, Ben Fielding and a young Chinese Christian Li Quan. They had trodden very different paths after separating following their shared student days at Yale University. Ben Fielding rose in the business world having little regard for Christian values while Li Quan paid a great cost for his Christian profession. The sufferings of the Chinese House Churches are vividly described and those of Li Quan in particular.

The climax comes with Li Quan's eventual influence on his friend Ben Fielding when they meet again after twenty years. But every now and then throughout the book we are given a glimpse into heaven and shown the perspective from which heaven views the events on earth and the sufferings of many faithful Christians. We see also its view of the worldliness of those who profess to be Christian but whose lives and interests betray their professions. This book had a strange influence on me, partly because of my childhood background and also because of the deep empathy I felt with the Chinese church for which my father had given his life in missionary endeavour.

Heaven

The name Randy Alcorn remained fixed in my mind and when I discovered he had written a book simply called *Heaven,* I was intrigued and bought a copy. A thorough and amazingly instructive book on the whole subject of the life to come and the new earth— our eventual home. I found it gripping—even exciting. Of course, some of the things that Alcorn says fall into the category of conjecture and he freely admits that this is the case. Again and again, however, just as I thought 'How can you possibly say that?' I found he had a Scripture reference to support his thinking. Picking up on verses such as Romans 8:19–23, he vividly shows how all creation is eagerly awaiting the day when God wraps up this poor, broken, sinning earth and brings in the new heavens and the new earth where we will live, breathe, serve the God of glory and enjoy everything that has been beautiful on this earth, but cleansed from all defilement—a splendid prospect.

Admittedly, the subject of the life to come is one that many Christians are reluctant to discuss. Some harbour secret fears of the unknown or prefer to take refuge in a 'wait and see' outlook backed up with such Scriptures as 1 Corinthians 2:9, 'No eye has seen nor ear heard ... what God has prepared for those that love him.'[43] Yet many of the great theologians of the past exhort us to meditate often on heaven. Richard Baxter, in *The Saints' Everlasting Rest*, urges us to let our minds frequently contemplate heaven, to 'walk' the streets of the New Jerusalem and 'visit' the many mansions prepared for us. He gives more than twenty-five pages of his book to help us in such meditation. Samuel Rutherford, John Owen, Jonathan Edwards, William Grimshaw all speak with one voice on the subject as do many others including C. S. Lewis, in his amazing description of the Real Narnia in *The Last Battle*—the final episode in *The Chronicles of Narnia* series.

The Dawn of Heaven Breaks

To allay our fears, I was delighted with the publication of Dr Sharon James's book of meditations on our future hope called *The Dawn of Heaven Breaks* with the subtitle *Anticipating Eternity*.[44] With a collection of extracts from the writings of a number of writers, passages from Scripture and hymns, this beautifully produced book addresses such subjects as illness, ageing, facing death and eternity.

The quotations Sharon James has chosen combine tenderness with boldness, and make appropriate reading for Christians of any age as they face times of illnesses and especially for those coping with the fear of death or the anxiety of losing those whom they have loved. Before many of the quotations we are given an explanatory paragraph to show the circumstances which prompted the words that were written.

One piece from the writings of John Bradford, martyred for his faith in 1555, is particularly moving. Queen Mary—known derogatively in history as Bloody Queen Mary—had scarcely been queen for one month before this good man was arrested on some trivial charge and thrown first into the Tower of London and then removed to the King's Bench Prison. For eighteen long months he languished in prison knowing that at any moment the jailer could enter his cell and summon him to the stake. Much of his time was spent in writing letters and meditating on heaven. One quotation from these letters is particularly poignant in the circumstances:

> I am assured that though I want here, I have riches there; though I hunger here, I shall have fullness there; though I faint here, I shall be refreshed there; and though I be accounted here as a dead man, I shall there live in perpetual glory … There is the light that shall never go out; there is the health that shall never be impaired; there is the glory that shall never be defaced, there is the life that shall taste no death.

At last in June 1555 it was the jailer's wife who hurried into his cell exclaiming, 'O Master Bradford, I come to bring you heavy news. Tomorrow you must be burnt and your chain is now a-buying.' Bradford's reply was typical of the man: 'I thank God for it … the Lord make me worthy thereof.' And the next day, as he was being chained to the stake in Smithfields, London, he encouraged his young fellow-sufferer, John Leaf, in memorable words: 'Be of good comfort, brother; for we shall have a merry supper with the Lord this night.'

Our final Challenge

An extract from a sermon by Alexander Maclaren is thought-provoking. Preaching on death itself, he takes the words of the apostle Paul: 'The time of my departure has come. I have fought the good fight, I have finished the course, I have kept the faith. Henceforth there is laid up for me the crown of righteousness which the Lord, the righteous judge will give me on that Day ...'

> If you can humbly say, 'For to me to live is Christ,' then it is well ... We may be ready quietly to lie down when the time comes and may have all the future filled with the blaze of a great hope that glows brighter as the darkness thickens. That peaceful hope will not leave us until consciousness fails. Then when it has ceased to guide us, Christ himself will lead us through the waters; when we open our half-bewildered eyes in brief wonder, the first thing we will see will be his welcoming smile. His voice will say, as a tender surgeon might to a little child waking after an operation, 'It is all over.'

In case Alexander Whyte's suggestion that *The Letters of Samuel Rutherford* should be tucked under the pillow of every dying Christian proves too bulky for comfort, then *The Dawn of Heaven Breaks* is a slim enough book to form an excellent alternative.

Isabella Graham was a Scottish woman who spent her last years in New York helping the widows of men struck down by the ravages of the Yellow Fever epidemics that hit the area during the late 1790s. Having witnessed so many sudden deaths, she gave much thought to the Christian's preparations for that final eventuality. In every other endeavour in life we may have a second chance to perform better if we fail the first time. But we have only one opportunity to die well. Knowing that so often in the extremity of illness it is scarcely possible to think clearly, Isabella prepared a *Book of Provisions against the Crossing of Jordan*. In this book she wrote down all the hymns, Scriptures, and quotations from other writers that she would like someone to read to her at the end. I too have tried to do the same but my notebook is lamentably short. That does not matter. Sharon James has done it for us and with this book at our bedside we may be comforted and sustained at the last.

Perhaps it would be appropriate to end this short study with a verse from a hymn that Paul and I chose for our wedding. It picks up the theme of Abraham who looked for 'a better country, that is a heavenly one'.

> The God of Abraham praise
> At whose supreme command
> From earth I rise and seek the joys
> At his right hand.

> I all on earth forsake—
> Its wisdom, fame and power—
> And him my only portion make,
> My shield and tower.

Endnotes

1. Annual publications of the Metropolitan Tabernacle monthly magazine. The title derives from Nehemiah's instructions that the men who were rebuilding the walls of Jerusalem were to do so with their trowels in one hand and their swords in the other to be instantly ready for any attack of the enemy (Nehemiah 4:17).

2. Ephesians 6:12.

3. Some versions include extra stanzas.

4. Many years later, one of these two, an honourable man, sent us a cheque for seven pounds, seven shillings and seven pence as a way of apologizing—an amount chosen to symbolize the scriptural number of 7 as perfection and completeness.

5. Now, as a dormitory town to Loughborough, its population is nearer 15,000.

6. This small book has been attractively republished by Evangelical Press in 2001 coupled with another of Bunyan's shorter works *The Narrow Gate* (the original title was *The Strait Gate*).

7. Bunyan was in prison when he started writing this book, but broke off in the middle as ideas for *The Pilgrim's Progress* came pouring into his mind.

8. David Charles, 1762–1834; trans. by Lewis Edwards, 1809–87.

9. Johann Frank, 1618–77; trans. by Catherine Winkworth, 1827–78.

10. Translated by Robert Maynard Jones (Bobi Jones).

11. *New Christian Hymns*, an updated and sympathetically modernized version of this book, containing many more of the new hymns of recent years, was published in 2004.

12. John F. MacArthur, *The Glory of Heaven*, Crossway Books, 1996, p. 123.

13. Kregel Publications, Grand Rapids, 1992.

14. IVP, 2013.

15. One new believer, converted at the time, had prayed that if there was a God he would show him a shooting star when he was walking the dog one night. He did! The man began to attend the church services and was truly converted. Although he had never before read a book in his life, he was found happily reading William Gurnall's massive work!

16. William Gurnall, p. 409.

17. The language in the Spurgeon quotes has been slightly updated.

18. *Metropolitan Tabernacle Pulpit*, vol. 13, p. 61 ff.

19. Gerhard Tersteegen.

20. 2 Corinthians 12:9.

21. Romans 8:32.

22. *Works* of Thomas Brooks, vol. 5, p. 569.

23. IVP, 2013.

24. Mark 3:35.

25. Julian Hardyman's penetrating and searching work, *Idols, God's battle for our hearts,* is one of the most helpful and convicting books on this subject. IVP, 1988.

26. Language slightly updated.

27. Slightly updated.

28. This has been beautifully republished by the Banner of Truth Trust, in *de luxe* binding.

29. I later wrote an article on Mitchell's life and when his daughter contacted me I felt it right that she should have her father's copy of the book.

30. Samuel Rutherford, *Letters*, Banner of Truth, 2006, p. 299.

31. *Letters* p. 41.

32. *Letters* p. 19.

33. Rutherford's *Letters,* p. 178.

34. John Bunyan, *Grace abounding to the chief of sinners* in *Works*, Banner of Truth, 1991, p. 43.

35. *Law and Grace unfolded*, vol. 1, p. 563.

36. Ibid. p. 550.

37. *Works*, vol. 1, p. 573. Wording slightly updated.

38. Ibid. vol. 1, p. 759.

39. Ibid. vol. 3, p. 243

40. *The Treasury of David*, vol. 1, p. 401.

41. *Grace and Glory*, Banner or Truth Trust, 1994.

42. Ibid.

43. It is important to remember that the following verse contains a strong conclusion to this statement, 'These things God has revealed to us through the Spirit.'

44. Sharon James, *The Dawn of Heaven Breaks*, EP, 2007.